Healing the Wounds of Military Trauma

Participant Book

"*Healing the Wounds of Military Trauma* is a critically needed tool, rooted in the Christian faith, that can help restore wholeness to those who have experienced trauma, moral injury, and isolation resulting from military service. It can also assist first responders who suffer trauma in the line of duty. The approach of this book is humble and holistic, honest and practical. It helps those who are hurting to cross over to healing. This book was needed yesterday, and I am so grateful to its authors, as well as the facilitators it will train up, who will help heal many."

Chris Seiple, Ph.D.
Former Marine Infantry Officer
President Emeritus, Institute for Global Engagement
Founder & CEO, The Sagestone Group

"For more than a decade I have been impressed by the genius and effectiveness of the original *Healing the Wounds of Trauma* materials. Now they have developed this edition for members of the military and their loved ones and, once again, I'm here to say I know of no other program that does a better job inviting hurting people into healing conversations with God and neighbor. The content has been contextualized to a military audience and lessons like 'Coming Home' and 'Moral Injury' address some of the unique challenges these families face. Read the book. Get the training. Consider how you might help others begin their healing journey."

Philip G. Monroe, Psy.D.
Psychologist and Founder, Global Trauma Recovery Institute
Trauma Healing Institute Advisory Council

"I am grateful for all the work that has gone into this much-needed book. It provides accurate and understandable information that can assist the global church in her work with the traumatized. The teaching is grounded in the Scriptures as well as in the professional literature about trauma. The suffering of traumatized people is clearly understood as is the care for those wounded in significant ways. The book speaks the truth about those wounds and also offers healing and hope. It is a precious gift to the body of Christ."

Diane Langberg, Ph.D.
Psychologist and author

Healing the Wounds of Military Trauma

Participant Book

Trauma Healing
INSTITUTE

HEALING THE WOUNDS OF MILITARY TRAUMA: PARTICIPANT BOOK

Based on *Healing the Wounds of Trauma: Participant Book* © 2021 SIL International and American Bible Society. Authors: Margaret Hill, Harriet Hill, Richard Baggé, and Pat Miersma. Editorial committee: Dana Ergenbright, Stacey Sutherland, Mary Crickmore, Bryan Varenkamp, Phil Monroe, and Debbie Wolcott.

Adapted for the military context by Pat Miersma (SIL), Stacey Sutherland (SIM), and Richard Baggé (SIL), with special thanks to David Garcia (SIL), Winona Cannady (SIL), Marilyn Davis (SIL), and Peter Edman (ABS) for significant help in reviewing, editing, and strengthening this edition.

Illustrations: Ian Dale
Typesetting and production: Peter Edman

ISBN (Paper)   978-1-58516-450-9 (ABS item 125645)
ISBN (Digital)   978-1-58516-451-6 (ABS item 125646)

For use with: *Healing the Wounds of Military Trauma: Facilitator Guide*

ISBN (Paper)   978-1-58516-448-6 (ABS item 125643)
ISBN (Digital)   978-1-58516-449-3 (ABS item 125644)

Trauma Healing Institute
101 North Independence Mall East FL8
Philadelphia, PA 19106

traumahealinginstitute.org

Printed in the United States of America

About the Program

In the world today, many people have experienced war, ethnic conflict, displacement, natural disasters, accidents, abuse, and crime. Many have been wounded inside by these things. The Church should be helping its members who are suffering (Acts 20:28), as well as being light and salt in the world. *Healing the Wounds of Military Trauma* is intended to help people recover from trauma and loss associated with the experiences of military members, veterans, and their families.

This program is an adaptation of *Healing the Wounds of Trauma: How the Church Can Help*, which was developed beginning in the late 1990s and first published in 2004 to help the local church respond to hurting people in a way that is helpful, rather than harmful. Each lesson presents what the Bible and mental health best practices teach about how to heal from trauma.

This product is not intended to diagnose, treat, or cure any disease. It does not take the place of professional counseling or psychiatric evaluation and treatment. If you use this product, you show that you understand this.

Contents

CORE LESSONS

1. What is a wound of the heart?

Section 1. Kris's story

Kris was standing at the sink washing dishes when she saw through the window two uniformed men get out of a car outside and walk toward the door. For a moment, she stood with her hands in the soapy water, frozen with fear. "Adam!" her mind screamed. "Something has happened to Adam!"

For eight months, Kris and the kids had been counting the days until his return from a year-long combat deployment. The doorbell rang and she walked slowly to open it, dreading what she would hear. She felt a mixture of fear and relief as the chaplain explained gently that Adam was alive, but that he had been severely wounded in an explosion that had killed his buddy Jimmy.

The days and weeks seemed to blur together for Kris until Adam finished several surgeries and rehab and came home. She tried to prepare the children, but they were still shocked to see their formerly strong father barely able to sit up in a wheelchair.

Still weak and dazed from pain, and embarrassed by the looks of pity on their faces, Adam quickly excused himself to the bedroom. He felt devastated and confused. He used to be so fit. Now he could think only about all the things he wasn't able to do. He felt like he was no longer the same person. Not physically and not even on the inside.

These days Kris is shocked at the change in her husband. Once an outgoing person, he now refuses to go out into the community or to church. He isolates himself at home and sometimes doesn't even want to see his platoon buddies when they visit. He used to be a loving, patient man, but now he gets angry at the slightest things and startles at every loud noise. He has been taking more and more of his pain medication even though his physical pain seems to be less and less. Now he takes his medicines just to sleep at night or to get through the day.

When the men from his squad come to visit, they do not seem to know what to say to Adam. They talk about the squad as if he will be coming back, though everyone knows he never will. Kris can see the hurt look in his eyes, but when she tries to talk to him about it, he angrily brushes her off. It worries Kris to see him so depressed, and she does not like the way he is angry at the kids. They are starting to avoid him. At night, Adam is waking up with terrible dreams and now Kris does not sleep well either.

Kris feels sad and alone. She knows the Bible says God can give us peace and joy, even in times of suffering. She keeps thinking about Isaiah 26:3, "You keep him in perfect peace whose mind is stayed on you, because he trusts in you." She believes it in her mind, but even though she prays and tries to trust in God, she does not feel any peace in her heart. That makes her feel like a bad Christian.

One day, her friend Grace comes by for a visit and Kris begins to share the pain that is in her heart. As Grace listens, Kris begins to cry and cannot stop. Grace listens to Kris explain what has been happening and how she feels. By the time Grace leaves, Kris feels like some of the burden is being lifted from her heart. They make plans to meet again the next week, and Grace encourages Kris to call her if she would just like to chat before they meet again.

DISCUSSION

1. Besides the loss of his physical health, what else has Adam lost?
2. What has Kris lost? What have the children lost?

Section 2. What is a wound of the heart?

Some experiences in life are very painful. They can cause deep suffering which often lasts a long time. This is what we call "trauma." Trauma is a deep wound of the heart and mind that takes a long time to heal. It hurts every part of our lives: how we relate to others, how our body feels, what we think about, and how much we can trust God. It can make us feel separated from God and others. We may feel like we are no longer the same person as before.

Trauma can be caused by a single event, a prolonged event, or repeated events. It overwhelms us with intense fear, helplessness, or horror, and often there is nothing we can do to stop it.

DISCUSSION

What types of events can cause trauma?

Our hearts can also be wounded, or traumatized, when we hear the details of someone else's experience of trauma, especially if that person is a family member or close friend. This is referred to as secondary trauma.

The diagram shows that trauma always involves loss, but we can experience loss and grief without trauma (for example, after the expected death of an elderly parent). Not all emotional pain is trauma, and not all problem behaviors are the result of trauma.

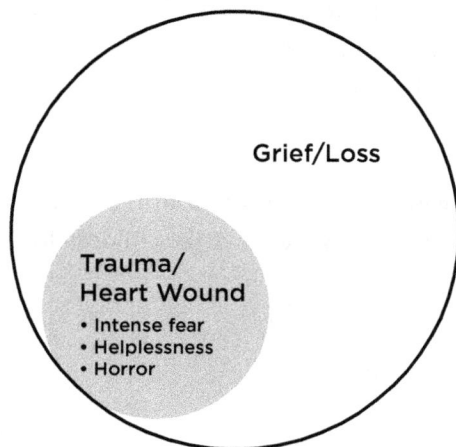

Grief/Loss

Trauma/
Heart Wound
• Intense fear
• Helplessness
• Horror

A. A heart wound is like a physical wound.

DISCUSSION

Think of a deep cut on your arm: What is it like? What helps it heal?

Now let's compare a physical wound to a heart wound.

PHYSICAL WOUND	HEART WOUND
It is **visible.**	It is invisible but shows up in the person's behavior.
It is **painful** and must be **treated with care.**	Same
If ignored, it is likely to get **worse.**	Same
It **must be cleaned** to remove any foreign objects or dirt.	The pain has to be expressed. If there is any sin, it must be confessed.
If a wound **heals on the surface** with infection still inside, it will cause the person to become very **sick.**	If people pretend their emotional wounds are healed when really they are not, it will often cause greater problems.
Only **God brings healing,** but often **uses people and medicine** to do so.	Same
If not treated, it often attracts **flies.**	Same. It often attracts bad things.
It **takes time to heal.**	Same
A healed wound **may leave a scar.**	Same. People can be healed, but they will not be exactly the same as before the wound.

B. How do people with wounded hearts behave?

When our hearts are wounded, it affects our lives. We may behave in three main ways: reliving the experience, avoiding reminders of the trauma, and being on alert all the time.

Reliving the experience

- Replaying the event or having "frozen images" in our minds.
- Feeling like "I can't get it out of my head/mind"
- Feeling like we are back in the event while awake (flashbacks) or asleep (nightmares)
- Telling everyone about what happened over and over

Any of these makes it hard to concentrate (at work or school).

Avoiding reminders of the trauma

- Trying to bury our feelings and not even think about the event
- Avoiding places, people, or other reminders of the event
- Going numb, such as not caring about what happens to us, not being disturbed by violence or by seeing dead bodies
- Not remembering what happened, or only remembering parts of it
- Using drugs, alcohol, pornography, work, food, or other addictive behaviors to avoid our feelings
- Completely refusing to talk about it

Being on alert all the time

- Always feeling tense, jumpy, frightened
- Living in dread of another bad thing happening
- Overreacting with violence or anger
- Struggling to fall asleep, waking in the night, or waking early in the morning
- Shaking, having a fast or irregular heartbeat

- Having headaches and stomachaches
- Feeling dizzy or faint, difficulty breathing, panic attacks.

C. What makes some wounds of the heart more serious?

Some situations are more difficult than others. For example:

- something that causes feelings of guilt or shame, the sense that we are bad or deeply flawed
- something that forces us to act in ways that go against our beliefs or feelings about what is right, especially if others have been harmed in the process (this is often called moral injury, and will be discussed in Lesson 2)
- something very personal, like a family member dying, or being betrayed by a close friend
- something that goes on for a long time
- something that happens many times over a period of time
- something that causes an unexpected death
- something done intentionally to cause us pain rather than something that is accidental

People react to painful events differently. Two people may go through the same event, but one may have a severe reaction while the other is not affected much at all. A person is likely to react more severely if he or she:

- has a mental illness or emotional problems
- is often sad or is highly sensitive
- had many bad things happen in the past, especially as a child, like being abused or having both parents die
- already had many problems before this happened
- did not have the support of family, friends, or operational group during and after the event

Section 3. What do our culture and the Bible teach us about expressing our feelings?

DISCUSSION
1. What does your military culture or your home culture teach people to do with their emotions when they are suffering inside?
2. What are some teachings Christians may hear in their groups about how they should handle painful feelings?

DISCUSSION
As you read the assigned verses, consider these questions:

1. What is happening?
2. How are people expressing their feelings?

Matthew 26:37–38 (Jesus)	John 11:33–35 (Jesus)
Matthew 26:75 (Peter)	Jonah 4:1–3 (Jonah)
1 Samuel 1:10, 13–16 (Hannah)	Psalm 55:4–6 (David)

Jesus had strong feelings and shared them with his disciples. Paul teaches us to share our problems with each other as a way of caring for each other (Galatians 6:2; Philippians 2:4). The Old Testament is full of examples of people pouring out their hearts to God: for example, Hannah, David, Solomon, Jeremiah. The psalmist tells God, "My heart is wounded within me" (Psalm 109:22b NIV). God wants us to be honest and speak the truth from our hearts (Psalm 15:1–2).

Keeping pain inside takes a lot of effort. It becomes harder to pay attention to our mission, the safety of our team, our spiritual life, and our families.

BREATHING EXERCISE

You have probably noticed that when you are upset or anxious, you may sigh. Sighing helps to relieve our tension. So too, choosing to breathe deeply can help us relax when we feel strong emotions. If this exercise makes you feel uncomfortable at any point, you can stop. You are in control.

- Get into a comfortable sitting position.
- Close your eyes if you like, or pick a spot on the wall and concentrate on it. Think only about your breathing.
- Slowly breathe in and out, filling your lungs and slowly releasing the air. Think to yourself, "(Your name), feel yourself relaxing as breath is flowing in and out."
- Think about being in a quiet place. It might be on the beach, or on a hill or under a tree. You might be alone or with someone who cares for you. You might think about Jesus telling you how much he loves you.
- Continue to think about your breathing, flowing in and out, in and out.
- After a few minutes, open your eyes or release your gaze from the spot on the wall. Stretch and take one more deep breath.

CLOSING

As you consider what stood out to you in this lesson about wounds of the heart, what is one thing you would like to remember for further thought?

2. What is moral injury?

Section 1. Two stories of moral injury

A. Joe's story

Joe was tense and alert. His combat unit was patrolling a volatile area and, as always, he felt responsible for his team's safety. Suddenly, they saw a teenage boy approaching from a distance. The boy waved and called out to them.

Joe was in front. He yelled out loudly, "Halt! Stop!" and pointed his weapon at the boy. "Stop, or we shoot!" Two other soldiers in his unit did the same, but the boy kept walking towards them with something in his hand. Joe felt time stand still. He knew he would have to shoot if the boy took one more step. But he was only a boy! His mind searched desperately for a way out. Again he screamed "Stop!" but the boy took another fateful step. Instinct and training kicked in. Joe discharged his weapon and the boy fell to the ground, dead, a pack of bread rolling from his limp hand.

The scene is still etched in Joe's mind and heart two years later. Joe has never shared the story with anyone, not even his priest. He struggles with guilt and shame. The horror of having taken an innocent life is constantly with him, but he never talks about it. Even though he had made the decision he was trained to make in that situation, he believes he is a terrible person. He can't face anyone, and he has pulled away from his friends and family. He cannot forgive himself and feels that even God cannot forgive him.

His own son, Paul, is thirteen now. Every time Joe looks at Paul, he feels a wave of pain. Even though he loves his son deeply, he finds himself withdrawing from him more and more. Joe doubts that he can be a good father to Paul. He wonders if his son would be better off without him.

DISCUSSION
1. What is Joe feeling about himself? About others? About God?
2. What might make it hard for Joe to recover from this event?

B. Josie's story

Josie realized she was going to be late picking her daughters up from the base school. "Not again!" she thought. The school had already warned her twice. She had been talking with members of her helicopter crew and lost track of time. She was also excited to get home so the kids could speak to their father, Scott. For the last six weeks he had been on special assignment and unable to communicate with his wife and children—until today.

She pulled the car onto the road and sped up, weaving in and out of traffic. She needed to make up time. This wasn't how she usually drove, but today was an exception. Both girls had soccer games later this evening. They would barely have time to make the call to their dad.

Her phone buzzed. Josie glanced down and saw an incoming text. Thinking it might be an important message from her husband, she looked back down and tapped the screen. Josie was a strong advocate against distracted driving, but after six weeks of waiting and wondering about her husband she thought she could manage this once.

Josie never saw the soldier walking to her right. As she looked down, her car drifted slightly, just enough to hit him and send him flying. Feeling the bump, Josie slammed on her brakes and pulled over. The car behind her had already stopped, and the driver ran over to the man's body. It was twisted. Josie approached and could immediately see that he was dead. She felt frozen in time. Everything slowed down. Someone pulled her away from the road.

Later, she remembered calling one of the crew members to get her girls. The military police came and covered the man's body with a sheet. They took statements from the other drivers. Josie, tears streaming down her face, told them the truth. She explained what a rush she had been in and how she had only looked down at her phone for a second. The officer shook his head.

When her husband called, she could hardly speak. He was given permission to return home, but it was another week before he arrived. The next days and weeks were a blur to her. She found herself weeping often and was unable to eat or sleep well. Once she found out that the young man had a wife and baby, Scott and the girls could not console her. Josie no longer wanted to attend church or get together with the women she had flown with. "If they knew what I've done and what a monster I am, they will hate me!" she said.

She cannot forgive herself and feels that even God cannot forgive her. At one point, Josie told her best friend Katie that she felt she could no longer live with herself. Katie went to Scott right away. "What should we do, Scott? I am so worried about Josie." Scott was concerned too. He had never seen Josie like this. She could no longer work, and she avoided time with the family. Her court date was coming up soon, and she did not seem to care what happened to her.

DISCUSSION
1. What is Josie feeling about herself? About others? About God?
2. What might make it hard for Josie to recover from this event?

Section 2. What is moral injury?

Many people describe moral injury as a type of "soul wound" that happens when a person believes or feels they have acted in ways that go against their deepest beliefs and values about what is right and good, and when others have been harmed as a result. It results in the person feeling deep guilt and shame. Moral injury may happen when people:

- feel forced to do something they believe is wrong.
- are prevented from doing something they believe is right and good.

- are in situations where there seem to be no good options to prevent harm or make the right choice.
- realize that they have acted in a way that violates their moral convictions.
- witness someone doing wrong or not doing right and they do not act to stop it.
- discover that the group they belong to, which they thought was doing good, is actually doing bad things and causing harm.
- feel they are to blame for others being harmed or dying.

When identifying moral injury, the focus is not on whether the action was sinful. They may not have actually done something wrong. Rather, the focus is on the kind of impact the action had on the person, or how they feel about it. They feel deeply guilty and shameful. They may feel that they cannot be forgiven.

DISCUSSION
1. What kinds of events could cause moral injury?
2. Have you known anyone who has suffered in this way?

Many events can cause moral injury. Common events are when a soldier kills or harms a civilian, a bystander fails to intervene when someone is being harmed, or a person supports an organization or system that ends up harming individuals.

As we saw earlier, *helplessness and horror* are often at the center of heart wounds. With a soul wound, the focus tends to be *guilt and shame* because of something the person did or thinks they did that felt deeply wrong. Moral injury needs special care for healing to take place, and even then, it may take a long time to heal. Many feel they are no longer the same person.

This diagram illustrates the relationship between moral injury, trauma, and grief. Not all traumatic experiences cause moral injury, and not all moral injury is caused by a traumatic experience. Trauma is a response to events or experiences that overwhelm one's normal ability to cope. This causes intense fear, a sense of helplessness, and horror. Moral injury is a type of trauma that results from the tension between one's beliefs or feelings about what is right and one's experiences and actions. It is characterized by guilt and especially shame.

Moral injury shows that a person is deeply grieved by the violation of what they believe or feel to be right and wrong. This is a healthier response than simply being indifferent.

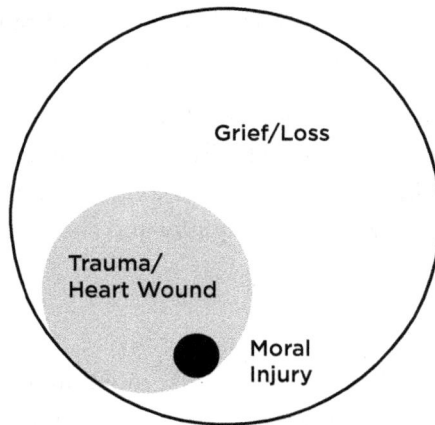

Section 3. What are the effects of moral injury?

People may not be aware they have a moral injury for some time after the event that causes it. Eventually, they begin to experience emotional pain from the deep guilt and shame. Guilt is feeling that we have *done* something we think is bad. Shame is the feeling that we *are* bad or deeply flawed.

Guilt and shame may be present in many heart wounds, but they are always present and especially deep and painful when a moral injury has occurred.

DISCUSSION

1. How do guilt and shame affect a person's life? Their relationship with God?
2. What are other effects of moral injury?

People with a moral injury may be angry at themselves for having done an evil thing. They may be angry at those who put them in the situation leading to moral injury. Or they may be angry at God for allowing such a terrible experience to happen. Suffering from a moral injury can lead people to lose hope.

They may feel unforgivable. Even if their actions would not lead to conviction in a court of law, they cannot forgive themselves. And they cannot imagine that God, their loved ones, or society will ever forgive them either. This can lead to isolation and loss of relationships.

Shame makes them want to hide, either physically or emotionally, never letting anyone know about the pain in their soul. They think that anyone who discovers what they did will abandon them, so they keep it secret.

Suffering from a moral injury can lead people to lose hope. They may:

- not be able to trust others.
- not be able to believe the Bible.
- not trust themselves to do what is good.
- try to avoid feeling any emotions so they will not have to feel the painful ones.
- despair to the point of trying to harm themselves or taking their own life.
- not be able to accept help that is offered to them.

Section 4. Moral injury and the Bible

The Bible does not use the term "moral injury," but it does describe many situations in which men and women suffered guilt and shame after they violated their deep sense of what was right, or they witnessed such a violation.

1.   In these examples, how might the characters have felt?

David	1 Samuel 22:17–22
Peter	Matthew 26:34–35, 69–75
Paul	Acts 8:1–3 and Acts 22:4–5

2.   How did God use them for his purposes afterwards?

David	2 Samuel 23:1–5
Peter	John 21:15–19
Paul	Acts 9:13–16; 1 Timothy 1:12–16

Each of these people may have felt grief, regret, hopelessness, guilt, and shame. They may have felt that God could never use them again for his good purposes. But God is always pursuing us. He loves us and desires a relationship with us and is ready to forgive when we turn to him.

In Matthew 26:69–75, Peter denied knowing Christ and then wept bitterly over his action. But later Jesus restored him (John 21:15–19), and God used him in greater ways for his purposes. Both David and Paul were the cause of harm to others, whether intentional or not. It grieved them deeply, but God did not give up on them. God always responds with grace to humble, repentant people (Isaiah 57:15; Psalm 51:17; James 4:6).

Some people may have feelings of deep guilt or shame about things that were not morally wrong. Healing for them will include coming to understand that though they did no wrong, their soul was still wounded.

Section 5. How can we help someone with moral injury?

DISCUSSION

1.   If you have known someone with this type of injury, was anything helpful for them? If yes, what?
2.   What was not helpful?

Here are some things that may help people with moral injury heal:

- Understanding what moral injury is and how it has impacted them. (Matthew 5:3–6)
- Discussing their story with someone they respect as a moral or spiritual leader. The listener should not try to minimize the person's feelings or rush to talk about forgiveness. (Psalm 32:1–5)
- Over time, if forgiveness is needed, forgiving themselves and others and beginning to accept the forgiveness God promises. (1 John 1:9)
- Reestablishing relationships with family and friends, making amends where necessary, and doing useful things for individuals and the community. (John 15:12–13; Isaiah 58:10–12)
- Participating in a community or church ceremony of forgiveness and reintegration. (Titus 3:4–8)

Moral injury may make it difficult for someone to reach out to others or receive help. What does the Bible teach us about receiving help from others?

DISCUSSION

Read these two stories of soldiers who needed help: Matthew 8:5–13 and 2 Kings 5:1–14. One needed help for someone he cared about and the other needed help for himself.

1. What prompted these people to seek healing?
2. Why might it have been difficult for them to ask for help?

In Matthew 8, the centurion sought help for his paralyzed servant who could not ask for himself. This required love and compassion, and Jesus calls him a man of great faith. Like this servant, hurting people may need intervention from others who care about them.

In 2 Kings 5, Naaman had to reveal his disease of leprosy to select people who could help him. This was difficult for him to do, but it led to healing. For those with heart wounds or moral injuries, it takes courage to name the event and the pain, but this is key to recovering.

What practical things can your church community do to help people heal from moral injury?

Churches should be places of healing for spiritually and emotionally wounded people. Churches can help by seeking out wounded people and inviting them into relationships where they are respected, loved, listened to, forgiven, and given opportunities to be involved in serving others. This can help them connect with others, which is an important part of healing both heart and soul wounds.

CLOSING

Close your eyes, if you like, and listen to these verses from the Bible. These things are true about everyone who is in Christ.

Zephaniah 3:17–18	2 Corinthians 5:17–19
Romans 5:8	Ephesians 2:8–10

What is one thing you want to remember from this lesson?

3. If God loves us, why do we suffer?

Section 1. Tim's story

Tim was a squad leader in his platoon. He never really knew his father, who was also a military serviceman. Tim's dad was distant and often away from the family for extended periods of time. Tim's parents finally divorced when he was eight years old. His mom remarried when he was ten, but Tim's new stepdad was cruel and beat him. He loved his mom, but he felt helpless and couldn't change things. As soon as he turned eighteen, Tim joined the service to get away from his stepdad.

Tim worked hard and moved up in rank. He seemed to be thriving in the military. It was a place where he felt he really belonged. As a young private, a buddy in his squad invited him to a chapel service. For the first time, Tim heard that Jesus died for him and he decided to become a Christian. Later, he married Sara, a girl from his newfound church, and they had two children. They were happy together.

But since coming home from combat, Tim finds himself becoming angry more easily and he finds himself avoiding friends and church. He doesn't look forward to going home at the end of the day, and when he is at home, he and Sara argue more and more. And now his second deployment is approaching and he dreads going back. He tries not to think too much about his last deployment. The platoon was hit hard, and he lost a close friend in the squad. He still misses Jimmy and thinks of him a lot. Another buddy, Adam, was severely wounded when an IED exploded. Tim had stepped over that same spot and he doesn't understand why Adam was hit but not him. He also saw many horrible things done to innocent civilians.

Tim still believes in the Bible, but he keeps asking why a loving God would allow so much suffering. He is angry with God and feels that God has deserted him. Sometimes he thinks that God doesn't hear his prayers or doesn't care enough to stop bad things from happening. Even though he knows God is supposed to be a loving Father, he can't imagine what that feels like. In his own experience, he only knew a father who was absent and a stepfather who beat him cruelly.

One day he begins to think about what he was taught in school as a kid—that God doesn't exist, that God did not create the world. Tim knows that this is not what the Bible teaches, but some part of him feels it might be true after all. Maybe there isn't a God listening to his prayers. He heard one preacher on the radio say that bad things happen to people because God is judging them for being sinful and doing bad things.

This only makes Tim feel more sad, lonely, and discouraged. At night, he reads a Bible story to his children and tells them God loves them, but inside he feels like a hypocrite, because he really feels that God is far away and uncaring.

DISCUSSION

1. What is Tim feeling in his heart about God?
2. In what other ways can people's ideas or feelings about God change because of suffering or trauma?
3. How have your own deployment experiences, or other suffering, affected your ideas or feelings about God?

Section 2. Why is there evil and suffering in the world?

Like Tim, when we suffer or see others suffer, we may have many questions about the evil and suffering in the world. These are questions that humans have asked since the beginning of time. The Bible begins with, "In the beginning God created the heavens and the earth" (Genesis 1:1), and then lists all that God created. When he finished, God looked over all he had made, and said it was very good (Genesis 1:31). If it was all "very good," what changed all that? Let's briefly discuss what the Bible says.

DISCUSSION

The Bible tells us some things about why there is evil and suffering in the world. Consider these passages: 1 Peter 5:8–9; Genesis 3:6–7; Genesis 3:17–18.

A. Satan

The Bible says that there is a supernatural evil being at work in the world, an enemy of God who is behind all wickedness (1 Peter 5:8–9; 1 John 3:8). He is a liar and a murderer who seeks to kill, steal, and destroy (John 8:44).

B. Choice

God created people with the freedom to choose good or evil. When Adam and Eve chose to disobey God, evil and death entered the world (Genesis 3:6–7). As a result, all of humanity now experiences sin and death (Romans 5:12). Sometimes we suffer from the choices of others, or from our own choices (Romans 3:10–12).

C. Damaged creation

Nature was impacted by Adam and Eve's disobedience (Genesis 3:17–18). The whole creation is marked by decay and pain, including such things as aging, illness, and natural disasters. While creation is still "very good," it groans to be set free from brokenness (Genesis 1:31; Romans 8:19–22).

DISCUSSION

If there was a risk of evil entering the world, why did God still give us choice?

Many people responding to this question over the years have suggested that God wants a relationship with people, not slaves; and that love requires giving the beloved choice.

Section 3. When we are suffering, what can make it hard to believe in God's love?

We have talked about why there is evil and suffering in the world and that God did not cause it. Yet even knowing this, we still struggle to make sense of our experience. Our pain and confusion can make us doubt God's love. Let's talk about why that might be.

A. Some cultural beliefs

DISCUSSION
1. What does your culture tell you God is like, especially in times of suffering?
2. What does your military culture tell you or imply that God is like, especially in times of suffering?

Some cultural beliefs are the same as what we learn from the Bible and help us through times of suffering. But other beliefs may be different, just like we saw in the story. These cultural beliefs may come to mind when we suffer and cause us to doubt God's love. Now let's look at what the Bible says.

DISCUSSION
What do these verses teach us about God in times of suffering?

2 Peter 3:9	Proverbs 6:16–19	Matthew 9:35–36
Psalm 34:18	Isaiah 53:3–4	Romans 8:35–39

God is all-powerful, but he is also patient. When we pray that God will stop a certain evil thing and it continues, we must not think it is because God is weak or does not care. He is in control and hears our prayers. He did not prevent the death of his Son on the cross. He is slow to act because he wants to give everyone time to repent (2 Peter 3:9). When the time is right, God will powerfully judge sin (Psalm 73:27).

    God hates evil and injustice. Not everything that happens is the perfect will of God (Proverbs 6:16–19; Genesis 6:5–6; Romans 1:18).

Jesus looks for us when we are suffering and has compassion on us. Jesus went looking for people who were suffering (Matthew 9:35–36). He preached the Good News and healed people of their diseases. He felt pity for them.

God comforts us. God is close to the brokenhearted and comforts us when we suffer (Psalm 34:18; 2 Corinthians 1:3–5). He holds us in his arms (Isaiah 40:11). He comforts us with his Word (Psalm 119:50, 92).

Jesus suffered and feels our pain. Jesus understands our suffering because he suffered on the cross (Isaiah 53:3–4; Matthew 27:46; Hebrews 12:2–3). He suffers with those who are suffering (Matthew 25:35–36).

God still loves us. Sometimes when trouble comes, we think it means that God does not love us anymore. This is not true. Nothing can separate us from his love (Romans 8:35–39). God promises to always be with us, even when we suffer (Psalm 23:4–5; Hebrews 13:5b–6; Isaiah 43:1–2).

B. Certain teachings

In addition to cultural beliefs, certain teachings can keep us from believing in God's love when we suffer.

DISCUSSION

1. Have you heard teachings about God that might make it hard to believe in God's love?

STATEMENT	COMPARE WITH
"God is angry when we sin and is quick to punish us with suffering."	Lamentations 3:22–23 1 John 4:9–11
"Suffering means we haven't done enough to please God. We need to earn his favor."	Romans 5:8 Titus 3:4–6
"Since God promises rewards for the righteous, when we suffer it means we did something wrong."	Philippians 1:29 2 Corinthians 1:8–10

2. What does the Bible say about these teachings?

"God is angry and quick to punish."

Compare with Lamentations 3:22–23 and 1 John 4:9–11. Some preaching makes us picture God in heaven as angry and wanting to punish us. The Bible tells us that God gets angry and punishes sin, but it also tells us of his great love for us (Jeremiah 31:3).

"Suffering means we have not done enough to please God."

Compare with Romans 5:8 and Titus 3:4–6. We may be told that we are suffering because we have not been good enough to please God. God's love is not based on our behavior. He loved us before we turned to him (1 John 4:19). He continues to love us by grace, not because of what we do (Romans 3:23–24; Ephesians 2:8–9).

"God promises prosperity for everyone who believes."

Compare with Philippians 1:29 and 2 Corinthians 1:8–10. If we are taught that people who obey God will always be rich and healthy, we may feel that we have caused our own suffering by our lack of obedience and faith. The apostle Paul is a good example of someone who suffered a lot, even though he was very obedient to God.

C. Certain experiences

Certain experiences in life can also make it hard for us to trust in God's love when we suffer. This is a common experience of God's people. Many of their stories are recorded in the Bible. Certain experiences we may have had in the church, or with our earthly parents or caregivers, might also affect our beliefs or feelings about God. In the military, some treatment by leaders can also affect our ability to trust authority figures.

1. If we have had challenging experiences with the church

Jesus commanded his followers to reflect the character of God, to challenge injustice, and to help those in need (Matthew 25:31–46; John 13:34–35; James 1:27).

DISCUSSION

> Let's read Matthew 5:13–16 for a description of how God's people should be.

When the church does not do its work, evil increases, and people may imagine that God is as unconcerned with injustice as those who claim to follow him (Matthew 5:13–16).

2. If we have had painful experiences with our earthly parents

Children need to feel secure and protected from evil. If we have experienced difficult things as a child, we may find it difficult to trust God when we become adults. For example, if we grew up without a father or mother, or if our caregiver was often angry with us, then we may think God has abandoned us or that he is always angry with us, even though the Bible teaches us that God is a loving Father (John 16:27; Romans 8:14–17).

Think about your own father. As a child, did you experience his love? Consider the same with your mother and other adults who took care of you. How does your experience with your earthly parents affect your experience with your heavenly Father?

DISCUSSION

In the story, we heard about some of these barriers to God's love—some cultural beliefs, certain teachings, and certain life and military experiences. Have any of these made it hard for you to trust that God loves you?

Section 4. How can we remember God's love in times of suffering?

DISCUSSION

We cannot explain why God allows us to suffer. Even if we could, it would not take away the pain. What can we do to help ourselves remember God's love in times of suffering?

A. Recognize when we have experienced God's help and presence in painful situations.

When we suffer or see others suffer, we can think about how God has helped us in the past. We can also think of how God has delivered his people in the Bible when they suffered (Psalm 107:6, 13, 19, 28). This can bring us comfort (Psalm 77:2–3, 11–12).

B. Do the things that make our faith grow.

As we follow Jesus and study the Bible, we learn the truth about God, and this helps us become free from the lies of Satan (John 8:31–32; 2 Timothy 3:14–17). Meeting with others for teaching, prayer, and fellowship (Acts

2:42; Hebrews 10:24–25). If these things are missing, we will find it much harder to believe in God's goodness when we suffer.

C. Meditate on God's character.

WORD ART ACTIVITY

What do you want to remember about God when you are suffering or watching someone else suffering?

- Take a piece of paper and write "God" in the middle of the page. Surround the word "God" with words or drawings that summarize the characteristics of God that you want to remember when there are times of suffering.
- In pairs, share as much of your word art as you would like, or share what it was like to do this activity.

EXPERIENCING GOD'S LOVE

It may be hard for you to receive love from God because of certain teachings and beliefs, relationships with caretakers, or other experiences. Relationships with earthly parents can be especially influential. But God's pure and genuine love will not harm you. As you reflect on these verses, they may help you get a better sense of how much God loves you.

Lamentations 3:21–24	1 John 3:1	Psalm 103:13
1 John 4:9–10	1 Peter 5:7	

CLOSING

What is one thing you want to remember from this lesson?

4. What can help our heart wounds heal?

Section 1. Jen and Paul's Story

Paul knew the minute Jen came home from work that it would be a bad night. He could never explain it, but Paul often felt the tension building before the explosion. No telling what might set it off, but they all knew it was coming. The whole family had learned to walk softly around her. She seemed anxious and tense all the time. Maybe it was from not sleeping, Paul thought. Jen had been plagued with terrible nightmares since returning from the war zone. She had been a field nurse at a medical unit close to the front lines. He knew she must have seen some horrible things. But no one could ask her questions about it—not even Paul. She just changed the subject.

Jen had been home over a year, but the Jen who came home was not the Jen who went to war. Paul did not understand the changes. All he knew was that he and the kids could not go on like this much longer. Even Jen seemed frustrated at her inability to contain the rage that filled her and spilled over on them.

She had also become very controlling, always worried about where the kids were and what they were doing. They were not allowed to spend time at their friends' homes, or play outside without Paul or Jen watching them, even though they were seven and nine. Paul hated feeling like their lives were governed by fear. But disagreeing only led to angry blow-ups. There was no reasoning with Jen or disagreeing on any issue, so Paul had stopped trying. When she got into a rage, she would say terrible things to him and the kids, and she often accused Paul of making her angry.

They still attended church as a family, but Paul could tell it was torture for her. She hated crowds. He had no idea what she was feeling. One day during an angry tirade Jen had thrown a glass dish across the room, cutting Paul's arm. She was immediately horrified at what she had done. Jen cried and begged Paul to forgive her. He held her in his arms and assured her that he did, but inside he was really worried. He didn't know how to help her.

A few days later, Jen's close friend Maria, who had just moved back to town, came to visit. As they chatted over coffee, Jen shared with Maria how terrible she felt about her outburst with Paul. She said, "I just feel so much rage inside. I know it's not Paul's fault. I just can't seem to stop being so angry. I never used to be this way before."

Maria replied, "I think you mean before deployment, right?" Jen nodded and Maria said, "It must have been so hard, Jen. Can you tell me some of what happened during that time?"

Jen began to share about the death and suffering she had seen. She also shared about times of being under attack. But when she told these stories, it sounded to Maria like Jen was reading them out of a book without any feelings. After a while, Maria reached out to touch her friend and said, "Jen, that sounds so sad to me. How did you feel when that was happening?"

Jen spoke again, slowly at first, and then tears came to her eyes as she remembered the feelings she had at the time. When she paused, Maria asked her, "What do you think was the hardest part for you, Jen?" Jen began to share more of her feelings, sometimes crying.

Over the next few weeks when Maria came to visit, she listened very carefully and closely to her friend. She let Jen go at her own pace and she didn't say much. She had never had an experience like Jen's, but she had a tender and peaceful spirit. Jen shared more and more of what had happened and how she felt. Being able to be heard was like a healing balm to Jen's hurting heart. As time went on, she felt lighter inside and less angry and tense.

DISCUSSION

1. What three questions did Maria ask Jen?
2. How did these questions help Jen?
3. What else did Maria do or say that was helpful to Jen?

Section 2. How can talking about our pain help us heal?

One way we get pain out of our hearts is by talking about it. In the Bible when people talk to God about their pain, this is sometimes called a lament. We will learn about this in our lesson on grief. Even if we talk to God about our bad experiences, telling another person about what happened is an important part of healing. As we share our pain with another person, little by little our reactions will become less and less intense. Sharing with a close friend, a pastor, or someone we trust can help a lot. For some it may be important to talk with a counselor. We may need to tell our story many times. But if we are not able to talk about our pain, and if there is no one to listen to us, these reactions may continue for months and even years.

A. What begins to happen when we talk about our pain?

When we talk with someone who listens well, it can help us:

- gain an honest understanding of what happened and how it has affected us.
- express our feelings about what happened.
- accept what happened.
- feel heard and know we are not alone.
- trust that God also wants to hear about our pain (Psalm 62:8).

B. What is a good listener like?

We can help each other heal by listening to each other. This requires that we become good listeners. What is a good listener like?

DISCUSSION

With what kind of person would you feel free to share your deep pain?

1. A good listener creates a safe space.

- Cares about you.
- Finds a safe and quiet place where you can talk without interruption.
- Does not force you to share more than you are comfortable sharing.
- Does not criticize you, preach at you, or give you quick solutions (Proverbs 18:13).
- Listens and understands your pain (Proverbs 20:5).
- Does not minimize your pain by comparing it with his or her own.
- Keeps the information confidential (Proverbs 11:13; 20:19).

2. A good listener asks helpful questions.

Here are three helpful questions a good listener might use:

LISTENING QUESTION	WHY IT HELPS
1. What happened?	It orients the listener and can lead into deeper discussion. It helps sort out facts and timeline, which can get mixed up in your brain during a traumatic event.
2. How did you feel?	Since healing takes place at the level of emotions, it helps to name them. Being heard with compassion can start the healing process.
3. What was the hardest part for you?	It can help both the person sharing and the listener to better understand the effects of the event. It also keeps the listener from thinking they already know the answer.

A good listener lets you speak at your own pace. You may give the answers to the questions without even being asked. Or, you may not be able to answer all the questions at one time. It may take several meetings to discuss the whole story and how it affected you.

3. A good listener shows he or she is listening.

- Looks at you (if that is good in the culture), not out the window or at their watch or phone.
- Does not seem impatient for you to finish.
- Gives encouragement, like saying "mm-hmm."
- From time to time, repeats what they think you have said so you can correct, restate, or affirm their understanding.

4. A good listener respects the healing process.

- Notices if you become very distressed. Lets you take a break, think about other things, and get calm inside. Allows you to resume telling your story when you feel ready.

- Understands that healing deep wounds takes time and may require several types of help. Knows that you may need to talk about your experience and the feelings it caused several times in order to heal.
- May ask if you would like prayer. If you say "yes," the listener prays, but does not preach. If you are not ready to pray together, the listener honors this.

C. What are signs that someone may need additional help?

Here are some signs that someone may need more help beyond spending time with a good listener:

- Their behaviors put life and health at risk.
- They are unable to complete daily activities or care for basic needs.
- They frequently cannot manage their emotions.
- They think things are happening that are not real, such as hearing voices or imagining that they are being followed.

These behaviors show that someone needs professional help. Try to connect them with medical and mental health professionals, if available, who can provide counseling or medications they may need. If necessary, call for emergency help.

LISTENING EXERCISE

We become good listeners by practicing. Even as we practice, we can help each other heal. We'll be listening in pairs. Each person can choose one painful thing to talk about that happened to them—this should be a small thing, not the worst thing they have experienced. The other person will use the three questions and listen to them. Then the listener and talker will switch roles.

1. What happened?
2. How did you feel?
3. What was the hardest part for you?

After listening to each other, discuss these questions:

1. How did you feel during this exercise?
2. Was anything difficult when you were the listener? Explain.
3. Was anything difficult when you were sharing? Explain.
4. What did the listener do well?

Section 3. How else can we express our pain?

Another way we can express the pain in our hearts is by doing activities such as drawing, poetry, dance, and music. Each of our cultures has different ways that people express themselves. We can use some of these ways to help find healing for our hearts.

ART EXERCISE

Start by getting quiet inside and asking God to show you the pain in your heart. It may be pain from something about your life today or something from the past. When you are ready, you can begin expressing your pain through an art form you choose. Your artistic expression may be symbolic rather than realistic. This exercise is not about showing artistic talent to others, but about expressing what is in your heart.

DISCUSSION

1. Share as much or as little as you like about what you have created. Or, if you prefer, share what the experience was like to express your pain in this way.
2. Did you realize anything new?
3. Pray for one another.

CLOSING

What is one thing you want to remember from this lesson?

5. What happens when someone is grieving?

Section 1. Miguel's story

"Medic! Medic!" Miguel could hear the frantic screams. After a moment of near-paralysis from the shock of the blast, his training took over and he sprinted toward his two fallen buddies. An IED had been triggered by the patrol team and two soldiers were down. Miguel prayed silently as he worked to assess their wounds. Both Jimmy and Adam were badly hurt. Miguel had to make a hard decision. It was obvious Jimmy would not make it. But Adam might, so he treated Adam first. Jimmy died of his wounds a few minutes later. Adam was airlifted to the nearest medical unit.

When Miguel returned to the base with the rest of the squad, everyone was silent. The chaplain met the team and talked quietly with each one. A couple of the guys actually wept, while one or two looked angry, kicking things around. But mostly they remained quiet, their faces set in grief and disbelief. Jimmy was gone. Jimmy, their laughing, smiling friend who always had a joke to tell, who had the whole world in front of him. He was only nineteen.

Later they went back on patrol. Chaplain Dave prayed for them before they left. He looked into Miguel's eyes and saw the confusion and guilt there. He made a mental note to check in with Miguel soon.

The deployment ended a few months later. Miguel still struggled with the guilt and anger of having to choose between treating Adam or Jimmy first. Back home, his squad mate, Emma, noticed that Miguel was drinking more than he used to. She spoke with him after he forgot some important duties, and Miguel told Emma that he was not sleeping well. She went to the chaplain and asked him what she could do to help her friend.

Chaplain Dave reminded Emma that it had only been four months since Jimmy died. Miguel was grieving, he said, and grief is like a journey that each person in the squad would experience differently. Dave said he would check on Miguel because drinking was not a healthy way to cope with grief. He gave Emma some ideas for how to listen to Miguel and be his friend, and told her that a memorial service was being planned for the battalion to honor Jimmy and other fallen soldiers. Jimmy's parents and fiancée would be invited. He asked Emma to consider sharing a memory about Jimmy during the service.

At the memorial service, Emma noticed that Miguel was not his usual quiet self. Instead, he was loud and slurring his words. When she got closer, she smelled alcohol on his breath. Quickly she took his arm and steered him out the back of the chapel. "What are you doing? How can you come here like this?" She shook him angrily.

Miguel sat down hard on the steps. He put his head in his hands. "I don't know, Emma. I just want the pain to go away."

DISCUSSION

1. What are the different ways the people in the story responded to this loss?
2. What are some common ways you've seen people in military communities respond to losses like this? Service members? Spouses? Children?

Section 2. What is grieving?

Grieving is feeling deep sorrow about the loss of someone or something. This might be the loss of a family member or a friend. It might be the loss of a body part or bodily function. It might be the loss of property or position or hope. Whether small or large, all losses affect us (Nehemiah 1:3–4). Grieving is the normal process of recovering from these losses.

Trauma always involves loss, but we can experience loss without trauma, as in the case of the slow death of an elderly parent.

When people lose someone or something very important to them, they may lose a sense of who they are. For example, they are no longer the wife of _____, or the mother of _____, or the leader of _____. Their life will never be the same. Through the grieving process, a person's former sense of who they are will change. This takes time.

Because Adam and Eve sinned, death and loss came into the world. Only in heaven will there be no more mourning (Revelation 21:4). Christians can grieve and have hope at the same time (1 Thessalonians 4:13).

INDIVIDUAL REFLECTION

What kinds of losses have you experienced?

Section 3. How can we grieve in a way that brings healing?

Grieving takes time and energy (Psalm 6:6–7). It is often like a journey that takes us through several neighborhoods. Each person spends different amounts of time in the neighborhoods and goes back and forth at different times. Understanding the grief journey does not take away the pain, but it can help us be more patient with ourselves and others. If we allow ourselves to take the journey, it will lead to healing.

A. The Neighborhood of Denial and Anger

Immediately after the traumatic loss the person or family is in Neighborhood 1, the neighborhood of Denial and Anger. This often lasts one month or longer. Right after a loss, denial and anger are natural and can actually be helpful:

- Denial allows us to absorb the loss little by little and keeps us from being overwhelmed by it.
- Anger can be a way of fighting against the loss when we feel helpless. It can give us energy and keep us from being overwhelmed.

Common responses:

- Feeling numb
- Unaware of what is happening around us
- Cannot believe the person has died or the event has happened
- May suddenly start to cry or erupt in anger

- Angry with God
- Angry with the person who has died, for leaving us alone
- Thinking or saying, "If only I had (done this or that), this would not have happened." or "I wish I had …"
- Asking, "Why did this happen to me?"
- May find someone to blame for the loss
- May take revenge, which results in conflict and more pain
- May think we hear or see the dead person

This stage can begin immediately after the loss or during the time of the funeral, and while people are still coming to comfort the bereaved family. Weeping and rituals of the wake and burial are often helpful.

B. The Neighborhood of No Hope

At some point in our journey we may begin to feel hopeless. We may be entering the neighborhood of No Hope. This often lasts between 6 and 15 months, although it can be different for each person. Neighborhood 2 is the darkest place in the grieving process. People do not expect anything good to follow.

Common responses:

- Sad and hopeless
- Unable to organize life
- Longing for the dead or departed person to come back
- Lonely
- Suicidal
- Guilty, even if there is no reason to be
- Avoiding the pain with drugs or other addictions

C. The Neighborhood of New Beginnings

At a certain point, we may come to Neighborhood 3, the neighborhood of New Beginnings. In Neighborhood 3, people increasingly accept the loss and their new identity. What is "normal" now is different—a "new normal." They may be more aware of what really matters in life. If they have grieved well, they may be able to help others.

Common responses:

- Thinking about moving on to a new life
- Ready to go out and enjoy time with friends
- Considering remarrying if a spouse died, or having another child if a child died
- Changed by the loss; may be stronger, more tender

D. The grief journey is not always direct

Everyone's grief journey can be different. Each individual spends different amounts of time in the neighborhoods and goes back and forth at different times. It is normal to revisit previous neighborhoods for short periods of time. Sometimes this happens in response to an event like the anniversary of a death. Gradually a person moves more and more into the Neighborhood of New Beginnings.

Sometimes people get stuck too long in Neighborhood 1 or 2 and may need special help to move on. Examples of this might be:

- A woman who still thinks she can see or hear her husband years after he died.
- A mother of a dead child who keeps his clothes ready for him and will not give them away, a year or more after the death.
- A man who is still unwilling to go to social events with his friends two years after his wife has died.

E. The False Bridge

Sometimes we think that since we believe the gospel and all the promises of God, it would be wrong to feel angry or sad about a loss. Our cultures may reinforce this idea. This can be called the "false bridge," because it appears to provide a shorter path from the moment of the loss directly to "New Beginnings," without passing through Neighborhoods 1 and 2. This is not biblical and it will not bring healing.

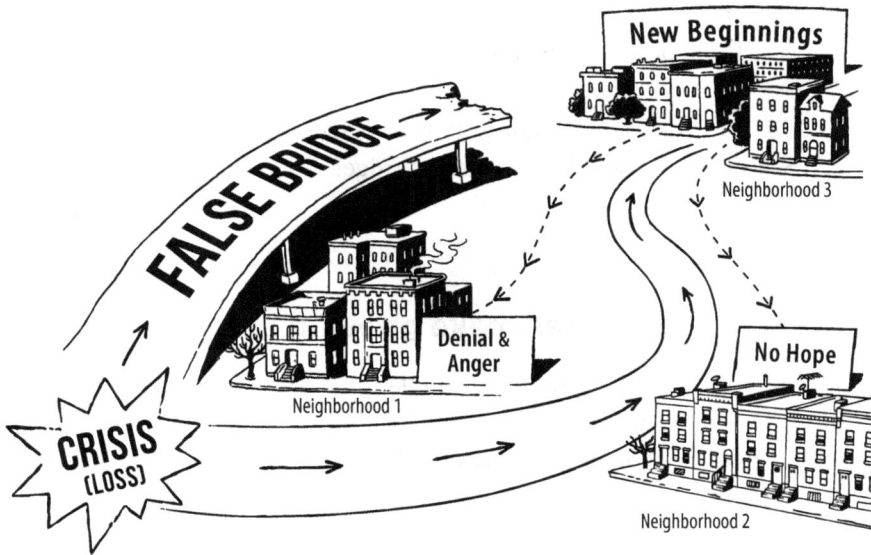

God made us with the need to grieve our losses. Jesus expressed painful emotions on the cross when he said, "My God, my God, why did you abandon me?" (Matthew 27:46). The psalmist cried to God day and night when he was in exile, remembering all he had lost (Psalm 42:3–6).

Facing the pain of loss takes courage. We are tempted to avoid it. Sometimes we get busy doing God's work as a way to avoid feeling the pain. But if we do not grieve a loss, the grief will stay in us and may cause problems for many years.

F. Sometimes the grief journey is delayed

Sometimes it is necessary to set aside grieving our losses in order to survive. The context might require us to just keep going or keep working, for example, because of responsibilities or because it is not safe to talk about the issue. When we are safe and life is stable again, we will need to take the grief journey. As we saw in the "Bottles under water" exercise, it takes effort to keep the emotions buried inside us.

DISCUSSION
1. Think of a loss you have experienced. What was your grief journey like?
2. Did you loop back or get stuck along the way?
3. Did you try to take the false bridge?
4. Did you have to delay the journey?

Section 4. What can make grieving more difficult?

Grieving is hard work, but some things can make it even more difficult. These can be things such as how the loss happened, beliefs people have about grief, and people who say or do things that show they do not understand.

A. The type of loss or context of loss

Some losses are especially difficult, such as when a child has died. What other types of losses are especially difficult?

- When there are many deaths or losses at the same time
- When the death or loss is sudden or violent, as with suicide or murder
- When there is no corpse to be buried or no way to confirm that the person has died
- When you are displaced and cannot participate in the grieving rituals
- When a provider or leader has died
- When the bereaved have unresolved problems with the dead person
- When a child has died
- When you are still in the midst of ongoing trauma (such as war)

B. Beliefs about weeping or the free expression of grief

DISCUSSION

1. What does military culture say about men weeping? About women weeping?
2. In what ways do these beliefs help or hinder people's grieving?

Some cultures require people to cry publicly when someone dies. Those who do not cry are suspected of not caring about the person who died, or of having caused the death. This can result in people crying dramatically, whether they feel sad or not.

Other cultures do not allow people to cry, especially men. This can result in people holding their grief inside rather than expressing it.

People should not hold their tears inside when the time is right for crying. The Bible says there is a "time to weep" (Ecclesiastes 3:4) God has designed us to cry or weep when we are sad. It is an important part of grieving, for men as well as women. Even Jesus wept when his close friend Lazarus died (John 11:33–38a). The psalmists wept (Psalm 6:6; Psalm 39:12; Psalm 42:3), as did the prophets (Isaiah 22:4; Jeremiah 9:1).

God notices our tears; they are precious to him (Isaiah 38:3–5; Psalm 56:8).

C. Miserable comforters

Sometimes well-meaning people try to comfort us, but it is not helpful. The story of Job gives a description of what it can be like.

DISCUSSION

1. Do you know the story of Job in the Bible? What do you remember about it?
2. What did Job's friends do or say that was helpful?
3. What did they do or say that was not helpful?

Job was a wealthy man with a large family. In an instant, he lost everything: his children, his cattle, his wealth, his health. When three of Job's friends heard what happened to him, they got together and went to comfort him (Job 2:11). They sat in silence with him for a week before speaking. When Job broke the silence and expressed his pain, his friends were quick to point out his lack of faith (Job 4:3–6). They said his suffering was due to his sins and the sins of his children (Job 4:7–8). Although Job claimed he had not sinned, they were sure that if he were innocent, God would not have let this happen (Job 8:6–8; 11:2–4; 22:21–30). They accused him over and over to try to get him to confess. Finally, Job said, "Miserable comforters are you all!" (Job 16:2 NIV). Rather than comforting Job, they increased his pain.

Section 5. How can we help each other grieve?

DISCUSSION

1. When you have been grieving the loss of someone or something, what sort of helpful things have people done or said? What sort of unhelpful things have been done or said?
2. How does your military or other culture traditionally help those who grieve? What customs are helpful? Which ones are not helpful? Which traditions are in keeping with Scripture?

Here are some ways we can help each other grieve:

A. Emotional help

- Visit the grieving person, when appropriate.
- When they are ready, encourage them to talk about how they feel. Allow them to express their anger and sadness.
- Listen to their pain. Do more listening than talking. They cannot absorb teaching and preaching at this time (Job 21:2; Proverbs 18:13).
- Help them to understand that it is normal to grieve, and that it is a process that will take time. They will not always feel like they do right now. It is important that they do not make major changes

based on how they feel as they go through Neighborhoods 1 and 2. When they are in Neighborhood 3, they will be able to make better decisions.

- When people are ready, you can pray with or for them (Ephesians 6:18). You can also read a promise from the Bible and encourage them to memorize it. For example: "The LORD is near to those who are discouraged; he saves those who have lost all hope." (Psalm 34:18).

- Eventually, they need to bring their pain to God. The more specific they can be about their loss, the better. For example, they may have lost a loved one, but also an income, companionship, respect, or security. They should bring these losses to God one by one.

B. Practical help

If a grieving person has to worry about caring for themselves and their family, they will not have enough energy to grieve properly and recover. They might be too exhausted to do the work they did before, much less to do all the things the deceased person did.

- Relieve them of their regular responsibilities so that they can grieve. Especially at the time of the funeral and burial, there are many practical ways to help a grieving person. Widows and orphans are in particular need of help, and we are instructed to care for them (James 1:27).

- If there is no corpse, arrange a service to remember the person's life and to publicly acknowledge their death. A photo of the person can take the place of the corpse. If the family is dispersed, those who are displaced or grieving from a distance can hold similar ceremonies.

- It is not unusual for a person to have difficulty sleeping in the early weeks and months after a loss. If people are not able to sleep, encourage them to get physical exercise. As appropriate, encourage them to take walks, do outdoor work, or get involved in sports. Getting physically tired can help them sleep better at night.

- If the person denies that their loved one has died, gently help them realize it in small ways. For example, help the person to disperse their loved one's personal belongings.
- Encourage the person to get medical or professional help as needed.

Laments

In Psalm 13:1, David asks, "How much longer will you forget me, Lord? Forever?" In verse 6, he says, "I will sing to you, O Lord, because you have been good to me." How can David say both of these things at the same time? They seem contradictory.

God has given us a tool to help us express our grief. It is called a lament. Many of the Psalms are laments. In a lament, people pour out their complaints to God in an effort to persuade him to act on their behalf, all the while stating their trust in him (Psalm 62:8). A lament can be composed by an individual or by a community.

Laments can have seven parts:

- Address to God ("O God")
- Review of God's faithfulness in the past
- **A complaint**
- A confession of sin or claim of innocence
- A request for help
- God's response (often not stated)
- A promise to praise God, or a statement of trust in God

Not all parts are present in each lament, and they are not always in the same order. But there is always a complaint.

Laments allow a person to fully express their grief, and even accuse God. This is often, but not always, followed by a statement of trust in God (see Psalm 88 and Lamentations). This combination makes for very powerful prayers. The grief is not hidden, but rather expressed openly to God. Laments encourage people to be honest with God, to speak the truth about their feelings and doubts. To lament to God is a sign of faith, not of doubt.

In a lament, people do not attempt to solve the problem themselves, but they cry to God for help. They look to God, not the enemy, as the one ultimately in control of the situation. They ask God to take action to bring justice rather than taking action themselves (Psalm 28:3–4).

Laments are well known in many communities. They are a good way to express deep emotions.

EXERCISE

1. Can you identify the parts of this lament?

Psalm 13

1   *How much longer will you forget me, Lord? Forever?*
    How much longer will you hide yourself from me?
2   *How long must I endure trouble?*
    How long will sorrow fill my heart day and night?
    How long will my enemies triumph over me?
3   *Look at me, O Lord my God, and answer me.*
    Restore my strength; don't let me die.
4   *Don't let my enemies say, "We have defeated him."*
    Don't let them gloat over my downfall.
5   *I rely on your constant love;*
    I will be glad because you will rescue me.
6   *I will sing to you, O Lord,*
    because you have been good to me.

2. Take some time to create a lament to God. Your lament could be a song, rap, poem, prayer, dance, or any creative way you wish to express your feelings to God. It does not have to include all parts of a lament, but it does need to have a complaint.

DISCUSSION

Share as much or as little as you would like of your lament. Or, if you would prefer, share what the process of writing a lament was like for you.

CLOSING

What is one thing you want to remember from this lesson?

6. Bringing our pain to the cross

Section 1. Jesus sets a woman free

Jesus had been asked to go and heal a young girl who was very ill. As he was on his way, there were people following and crowding around him. A woman in the crowd had suffered for twelve years with constant bleeding. She had suffered a great deal from many doctors, and over the years she had spent everything she had to pay them, but she had gotten no better. In fact, she had gotten worse. She had heard about Jesus, so she came up behind him through the crowd and touched his robe. She thought, "If I can just touch his robe, I will be healed." Immediately the bleeding stopped, and she could feel in her body that she had been healed of her terrible condition.

Jesus realized at once that healing power had gone out from him, so he turned around in the crowd and asked, "Who touched my robe?"

His disciples said to him, "Look at this crowd pressing around you. How can you ask, 'Who touched me?'"

But he kept on looking around to see who had done it. Then the frightened woman, trembling at the realization of what had happened to her, came and fell to her knees in front of him. The whole crowd heard her explain why she had touched him and that she had been immediately healed. Jesus said to her, "Daughter, your faith has made you well. Go in peace. Your suffering is over."

(Adapted from Mark 5:25–34 NLT)

1. How would you describe this woman?
2. What happened when she touched Jesus?
3. Why do you think Jesus did not just let her disappear into the crowd?
4. How did she think Jesus would respond to her when she told the whole truth of her story? How did he respond?

INDIVIDUAL REFLECTION
1. Have you ever felt ashamed of your story?
2. How do you think Jesus would respond if you told him the whole truth of your story?

Section 2. Identify the wounds of your heart

Just as the person in the story took their pain to Jesus, we can do the same. We are taught in Scripture that Jesus came not only to bear our sins, but also to bear our pain and heal us. The Gospel of Matthew quotes the prophet Isaiah to describe what Jesus did: "He took our sickness and carried away our diseases" (Matthew 8:17, quoting Isaiah 53:4). In the same passage from the prophet Isaiah, it also says:

> *He was despised and rejected by mankind,*
> *a man of suffering, and familiar with pain.*
> *Like one from whom people hide their faces he was despised,*
> *and we held him in low esteem.*
> *But he was pierced for our transgressions,*
> *he was crushed for our iniquities;*
> *The punishment that brought us peace was on him,*
> *and by his wounds we are healed.*

(*Isaiah 53:3, 5 NIV*)

Jesus felt the full burden of human pain and sinfulness. Jesus knows the pain that is in our hearts, and we need to bring it to him so he can heal us.

TIME ALONE

Now we would like you to take some time alone and reflect on the pain(s) you want to bring to Jesus for healing. Write on the paper we have given you the things that give you pain—things done to you or things that you have done, left undone, or witnessed that may have created a wound for you. If you prefer, you can draw a picture or create some other way of expressing the pain. Please feel free now to find a quiet place alone, and we will call you back to this place afterward.

DISCUSSION

We will now give you an opportunity to share these pains with another person. You may share as much or as little as you like of what you have put on your paper. Or you may share what the experience of writing it was like. After sharing, take time to pray for each other. If you are not comfortable sharing what is in your heart, you can simply pray together.

Section 3. Bring your pain to Jesus

Jesus said, "Come to me, all of you who are tired from carrying heavy loads, and I will give you rest. Take my yoke and put it on you, and learn from me, because I am gentle and humble in spirit; and you will find rest" (Matthew 11:28–29).

Jesus invites you to come to him. When you are ready, you can bring your papers to the cross. If you would like, you can say, "I am bringing my pain to Jesus and asking him for healing." Feel free to linger at the cross as long as you need.

You may also have your hands washed. This is not a magic cleansing of your soul wound but a symbolic reminder that our sins are washed away when we receive God's forgiveness.

If you are not ready to bring your paper to the cross, feel free to stay where you are.

TIME TO BRING OUR PAIN TO JESUS

By destroying our papers, we are asking Jesus to take our suffering and continue to lead us on a journey of healing. Again, this is not magic. It is something we do with our whole body that helps our heart and mind understand that we are asking Jesus to take our pain.

In Luke 4, Jesus read part of the following passage and helped people understand that it refers to himself.

Isaiah 61:1–4

> *The Sovereign Lord has filled me with his Spirit.*
> *He has chosen me and sent me to bring good news to the poor,*
> *To heal the broken-hearted,*
> *To announce release to captives and freedom to those in prison.*
> *He has sent me to proclaim that the time has come*
> *When the Lord will save his people and defeat their enemies.*
> *He has sent me to comfort all who mourn,*
> *To give to those who mourn in Zion Joy and gladness instead of grief,*
> *A song of praise instead of sorrow.*
> *They will be like trees that the Lord himself has planted.*
> *They will all do what is right,*
> > *and God will be praised for what he has done.*
> *They will rebuild cities that have long been in ruins.*

Revelation 21:1–5

> *Then I saw a new heaven and a new earth. The first heaven and the first earth disappeared, and the sea vanished. And I saw the Holy City, the new Jerusalem, coming down out of heaven from God, prepared and ready, like a bride dressed to meet her husband. I heard a loud voice*

speaking from the throne: "Now God's home is with people! He will live with them, and they shall be his people. God himself will be with them, and he will be their God. He will wipe away all tears from their eyes. There will be no more death, no more grief or crying or pain. The old things have disappeared."

Then the one who sits on the throne said, "And now I make all things new!" He also said to me, "Write this, because these words are true and can be trusted."

CLOSING

Is there anything you want to share about what God has done for you during our time together?

7. How can we forgive others?

Section 1. Mateo's story

Mateo could still remember the shock and disbelief he felt as he read the email from his wife Laura. They had fought again, during a rare phone call. He got the email the next day. Just two months before his deployment ended, she had decided to take the children and move out. She said she could not endure the arguments and constant separations any longer. She needed time away, maybe permanently. He didn't have any spare energy to deal with his feelings, but he could not get her betrayal out of his mind.

He was never home for long, that was true. When he was home, their relationship was often troubled. Mateo had been deployed many times over the years, and he always found it difficult to fit back in whenever he returned. Yet somehow they had made it work.

Those last eight weeks of the deployment were the toughest of his life. Mateo struggled to contain his feelings. He did not want to appear weak in front of his squad—after all, he was in charge. They needed him to be strong. At night, alone, he grieved the state of his marriage. What would happen to their family now? Rage filled him too. How could Laura do this? How could she turn away from so many years together? And in the middle of such a tough posting!

By the time the deployment ended, Mateo had lost weight and he wasn't sleeping well. His attention to work was not good, and he found himself becoming critical and angry with everyone. All he could think of was the hurt and rejection. After he got home, Laura approached him to consider seeing a counselor together, but Mateo blew up at her again.

He felt defeated and wondered if his marriage would survive. He went to visit the chaplain for help.

Chaplain Dave listened carefully to Mateo's story and sat with him as he wept. He explained to Mateo that it is normal to find it hard to forgive when we feel rejected. But he also explained that by not letting go of our anger and hurt, it can become an ongoing source of bitterness and pain. God could help Mateo let go of his anger and help him to forgive. It would not be easy, but it would be important to begin healing his marriage. Chaplain Dave told Mateo he would be there to help them through the process, and they prayed together.

When Mateo left, he felt like some of the weight had been taken off his heart. He realized that he wanted to be able to forgive Laura. And he considered that maybe there were things he needed to ask her forgiveness for. He knew it would be difficult, but he began to think that maybe he and Laura could save their marriage. He began to feel some hope.

DISCUSSION

1. How was Mateo's lack of forgiveness affecting him? His thoughts? Feelings? Behaviors?
2. What things made it difficult for Mateo to forgive Laura?
3. What did Chaplain Dave do or say that you think was helpful to Mateo?

Section 2. What is forgiveness and what is it not?

DISCUSSION

What are some common sayings about forgiveness in your culture?

These are statements some people believe are true while others disagree. Let's talk about them and see what you all think.

- Forgiveness is saying the offense didn't matter or that we were not hurt by what the person did.

- Forgiveness involves a decision but may also take time to be felt at the heart level.
- Forgiveness is acting as if the event never happened.
- Forgiveness is understanding why the person did what he or she did.
- Forgiveness is not dependent on the offender apologizing first or changing his or her behavior.
- Forgiveness means that we will forget what happened.
- Forgiveness is not the same thing as reconciliation.
- Forgiveness means I will completely trust the person I have forgiven.
- Forgiveness means there will be no consequences for the action.
- Forgiveness does not mean letting the offender hurt us or other innocent people again.

DISCUSSION

We see that there are varying opinions about these things. In this lesson we're going to talk more about them and look at some Scripture verses to see what God has to say. It will be interesting to see if you end up with the same views at the end of the lesson.

Section 3. How can we forgive others?

If we think forgiving is too hard for us to do, we are right. But God can give us the strength to do all things (Philippians 4:13). Let's look at some of what the Bible says about forgiveness.

DISCUSSION

What do these passages teach us about forgiveness?

| Psalm 6:2–3, 6–7 Luke 18:31–33 | How could bringing our pain to Jesus help us forgive? |
| Acts 7:59–60 Romans 12:17–19 | How do we forgive if someone has not asked for forgiveness? |

Romans 13:1–4 Numbers 5:5–7	What is the relationship between forgiveness and consequences?
2 Corinthians 7:9–11	What signs does a person show when they have truly repented?

A. Be honest about the pain and bring it to Jesus

Forgiving someone means that we recognize that the person has wronged us, and we accept the pain their sin has caused us. We do not minimize the pain but, like the psalmist, we are honest with God about what we are feeling (Psalm 6:2–3, 6–7).

Our pain may last a long time, but we continue to bring it to Jesus, who understands the pain of being wronged by others (Luke 18:31–33; Isaiah 53:3). As Jesus heals us, then we will be able to begin to forgive those who have hurt us.

B. Release the offender to God without waiting for them to apologize

Often, we are unwilling to forgive until the offender has apologized to us. Or we want to see that the person has changed their behavior before we forgive them. However, Jesus and Stephen asked God to forgive the people who were killing them (Acts 7:59–60; Luke 23:34).

When we forgive, we release the offender and our wish for their harm to God. Instead of paying the person back, we put them into God's hands (Romans 12:17–19). We let go of our own right to judge and allow God to do so, knowing that he will judge with justice and righteousness (Psalm 9:8).

C. Let the offender face the consequences of their actions

Forgiving someone does not mean that they should not be punished if they have done wrong things. Even though we have forgiven someone, it may be necessary to bring them to justice to prevent them from hurting others in the future and to give them the opportunity to repent.

God has given national and traditional leaders the job of punishing criminals and protecting the innocent (Romans 13:1–4). God has charged church leaders to protect the innocent, too. They should never ignore or cover up sin but need to address it honestly (Proverbs 18:5; Ephesians 5:11; Galatians 6:1).

Forgiveness does not mean that the offender is excused from paying back what was taken. Some things can never be repaid. But if someone has stolen something, for example, the thief should return or replace it (Numbers 5:5–7; Philemon 18–19).

D. Determine if and when you are able to trust the offender again

Forgiveness is not the same thing as reconciliation. If we forgive someone, it does not mean that we trust him or her immediately. Just because we have forgiven a person does not mean that we are reconciled to them. It also does not mean that he or she has changed. Even if there is a change, trust has been broken and will take time to rebuild.

If we observe signs of true repentance in the person, we can consider beginning to trust them again (2 Corinthians 7:9–11). But it may take a long time before we can trust him or her completely. In some cases, it may never be safe to trust the person again. Before trusting his brothers, Joseph put them through some tests when they came to Egypt, to see whether they had changed (Genesis 42—44).

Forgiveness can open the way for our relationship with a person to be restored. It may cause the offender to repent and reconcile. But they may not choose to be reconciled to us. Even if we want a relationship to be restored, it requires action by both parties. Reconciliation is not always appropriate, for example, in certain cases of abuse.

Consider whether other wounds you carry may be making it harder for you to forgive someone. If you find things in your own life are blocking you, seek help in addressing those.

E. Allow time for the process

Forgiveness does not happen all at once. We decide to forgive, but sometimes as we remember the offense, we go back to feeling bitter. When this happens, we need to continue to take the pain to Jesus and reaffirm our commitment to forgive again.

The commitment to forgive often comes before we experience any feelings of forgiveness—some- times long before. Like the bird in the diagram, we may circle back many times in our hearts toward the "cage" of the offense. As we forgive again and again, eventually we will feel less pain when we remember the event. Just like the bird flies higher and farther from the cage, toward freedom, we move increasingly toward freedom each time we renew our commitment to forgive.

The cycle of forgiveness

Freedom

The 'cage'
of the offense

Conclusion

Forgiveness is a decision to release our right to pay back the offender. It acknowledges what has happened and how it has affected us. It is an ongoing process of reaffirming our decision to let go each time we remember the offense. It does not require us to trust the person again, nor release them from the consequences of the offense.

Section 4. Why should we forgive other people?

DISCUSSION

What do these verses say about why we should forgive?

Ephesians 4:26–27	2 Corinthians 2:10–11	Hebrews 12:14–15
Matthew 6:12	Ephesians 4:32	Matthew 18:21–35

Forgiveness sets us free

A. Forgiveness frees us from anger and bitterness.

It is appropriate for us to feel angry when we have been sinned against. But if we let our anger lead us to sin or if we let it fester, we can give Satan a foothold in our hearts (Ephesians 4:26–27; 2 Corinthians 2:10–11). We become slaves of anger and bitterness and they begin to destroy us. If we do not forgive someone who has offended us, we are the ones who suffer. Refusing to forgive can make us physically ill with headaches, stomach ulcers, or heart problems. It may make us become as violent and evil as those who offended us. Forgiveness releases us from all this.

If we do not forgive others, we can pass our bitterness on to our children. This poison will result in cycles of revenge and violence between groups which can go on for generations (Hebrews 12:14–15). Only forgiveness can break this cycle of revenge.

B. Forgiveness shows that we understand how much God has forgiven us.

When we understand how much we owe God because of our sins (Matthew 18:21–35), and how he has forgiven our debt through Jesus (Ephesians 4:32), we will want to extend that same forgiveness to others. But if we refuse to forgive others, it shows we do not understand how much we owe God and how much he has forgiven us (Matthew 6:12).

DISCUSSION
1. What traditions do you have that help you to forgive others? What traditions do you have that hinder you from forgiving?
2. What do you find the hardest thing about forgiving someone? What has helped you the most to forgive others?

Section 5. What if we are the ones who have caused the offense?

DISCUSSION
How can we repent? What does the Bible tell us?

James 4:8–10	1 John 1:9	Acts 26:20
Proverbs 28:13	James 5:16	Numbers 5:5–7

A. How can we repent?

- We allow God's Spirit to show us how much our sin hurts him and others. This may make us sad and even weep (James 4:8–9). This sorrow can be good for us. "For the kind of sorrow God wants us to experience leads us away from sin and results in salvation. There's no regret for that kind of sorrow. But worldly sorrow, which lacks repentance, results in spiritual death" (2 Corinthians 7:10 NLT). Both Peter and Judas were sad that they had denied Jesus, but Peter's sorrow brought him closer to God; Judas's led him to kill himself.
- We take responsibility for what we have done and clearly state our sin (Proverbs 28:13; Psalm 32:3–5).
- We are willing to listen to the person we have hurt express the pain we have caused.
- We seek God's forgiveness of our sin, and then accept that he has done so (1 John 1:9).
- We ask those we have offended to forgive us, without defending ourselves, blaming them, or demanding that they trust us again right away (James 5:16). We should ask forgiveness in such a way that all those affected by our sin are aware of our repentance. For example, if we insulted someone in front of others, then we should ask forgiveness in front of the other people as well.
- If we have repented in our hearts, we will show it by the way we act (Acts 26:20b).
- Repentance may involve paying back what was taken (Numbers 5:5–7).

B. How can we forgive ourselves?

DISCUSSION

1. Some people continue to feel guilt, shame, and regret even after doing all they should to repent and make restoration. Why do you think this is?

Many people find it difficult to forgive themselves, or to feel God's forgiveness. We can ask him to help us experience the truth that he has forgiven us. He has removed our sins from us as far as the east is from the west (1 John 1:9; Psalm 103:2–3, 11–12). Even though we may believe what the Bible says about God's forgiveness, we may need other people to help us through the process of accepting God's forgiveness. This could be a trusted pastor, counselor, or friend. This process can take time and the roots of our struggle can be deep. There may be consequences for our actions, and trust may need to be rebuilt with self and others. With time, however, we can experience the truth that God has forgiven us.

2. What do you find to be the hardest thing about forgiving yourself? What has helped you the most to forgive yourself?

Closing

1. Ask God to show you any sins of which you need to repent. Confess the sins to God and receive his forgiveness.
2. Ask God to show you any people you need to forgive. Ask him to help you forgive those people.

   If we confess our sins to God, he will keep his promise and do what is right: he will forgive us our sins and purify us from all our wrongdoing. (1 John 1:9)

3. What is one thing you want to remember from this lesson?

8. How can we look back and move forward with resilience?

Section 1. Karen's story

Karen was being sent to a deploying unit. Again. She read the orders with a feeling of dread. Her unit was due to leave in only a few months, and they might be gone for an entire year. How could she bear it? And how would she tell Steve and the girls? She closed her eyes and remembered her last deployment.

Karen was a nurse, and nurses were badly needed at the front. No amount of training could have prepared Karen for what she encountered. The terrible injuries of the soldiers, the lack of supplies, the frustration of feeling she could never do enough … and most of all, the children. The children were innocent casualties and sometimes pawns in the war. They were brought in with terrible injuries, sometimes the results of her own battalion's attacks. These children had been used or punished by the enemy Karen had come to loathe.

During her last deployment, Karen had found it difficult to sleep because of nightmares. She began to worry about the children and coming back home. She had grown up in church and was taught that God is all-powerful and benevolent. He wanted people to be happy and good. Before experiencing war, she believed that God answered prayer in the same way a chemist fills a prescription. You turn in the prayer-room request and it would be filled. So if she prayed for her family, God would protect them. But on the front line, she prayed fervently for God to protect the children and end the war, yet the war continued, and the children still came—broken and battered and dying. Her faith was shaken. She was angry at God.

One day, something had switched off inside her. She felt numb. Deep in her heart, Karen felt like God had abandoned her. She stopped reading her Bible and attending chapel, and she stopped praying. She could not pray to a God she did not understand and who seemed so far away. She felt betrayed and alone.

When she returned home after that deployment, she struggled to adapt. She still could not sleep well. She began to lash out at Steve and the girls. After a while, she and Steve sought counseling. She also visited with the chaplain and began attending the small Bible study he was leading with other veterans. It was a safe place where she could ask hard questions about God and begin to share some of her deeper feelings.

Slowly, Karen felt herself growing stronger emotionally and spiritually. She often went on long walks to pray. She understood God had not abandoned her, but that he would not fit into the same ideas she had of him before.

Now the news that she would be going on another deployment filled her with dread. What if this new, deeper faith also crumbled when it was confronted with the horrors she might experience? How could it be different this time?

DISCUSSION

1. How did Karen's first deployment affect her experience with God?
2. What things helped her begin to heal?

Section 2. How does God use suffering in our lives?

A. The healing experience

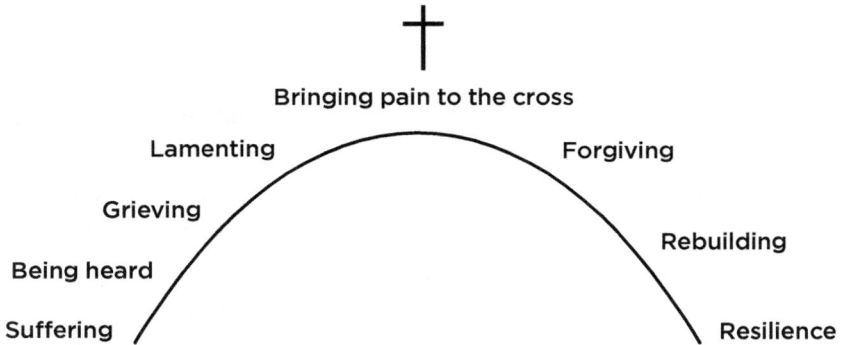

Healing from heart wounds is a process. Though it may be painful, going through the process is part of healing well. We have learned several parts of that process—remembering God's love, expressing our pain through words and art, grieving, lamenting, bringing our pain to the cross, and forgiving. When our wounds are deep, these are practices that God will use over time to continue healing our hearts.

These are also things we can do when we face new difficulties in our lives. As we practice these things, we will be able to rebuild our lives and be better able to face suffering in the future. This is called resilience. We will have good days and bad days—it is all part of the journey. And as we learned in our time together, we can talk to God at every step.

B. How God uses suffering in people's lives

DISCUSSION

Read aloud the Scripture passages below, then answer this question: What do these verses tell us about how God uses suffering in our lives?

Isaiah 40:11	Romans 5:3–5
2 Corinthians 1:3–5	1 Peter 1:6–7
Genesis 50:18–20	2 Corinthians 4:16–18
Romans 8:28–29	Isaiah 65:17, 25

God comforts us in our suffering so we can comfort others. God comforts us when we suffer. He holds us in his arms (Isaiah 40:11). He comforts us with his Word (Psalm 119:50, 92). We can pass on this same comfort to others when they suffer (2 Corinthians 1:3–5).

God works so that good comes out of evil. Joseph's brothers sold him into slavery, but God used this experience to deliver the Israelites from famine (Genesis 50:18–20). God turned the greatest evil ever done into the greatest good for us all when Jesus was crucified on the cross (Acts 3:13–15; Philippians 2:8–11). God works in ways we do not always understand, but we can always trust him to bring good ultimately, even if we do not see it in our lifetime (Romans 8:28–29; 11:33–36).

God uses suffering to strengthen our faith. Suffering strengthens our faith if we let it, and increases our ability to endure (Romans 5:3–5; James 1:2–4). Suffering is like fire: it is painful, but it results in purifying our faith in God. When gold is heated over a very hot fire, the bits of dirt in it rise to the top. These can be skimmed off, leaving pure gold (1 Peter 1:6–7).

God uses suffering to point us to the new heavens and new earth. When we suffer, we can think about the eternal kingdom that God is preparing for us (2 Corinthians 4:16–18), when Satan will be defeated (Revelation 20:10) and God will bring an end to evil and suffering (Isaiah 65:17, 25; Revelation 21:1–5).

DISCUSSION

How has God used suffering in your life?

Section 3. Moving forward: Practical tools for building resilience

God is present with us on our healing journey. Along the way, he is helping us build a strong foundation for our lives that will strengthen our resilience for what is ahead. In Matthew 7:24–27 Jesus tells a story about two houses. One was built on sand and collapsed when the storms came and the rain fell. The other house was built on rock and stood firm through the roughest weather. When we build our lives on Christ, we are laying a solid foundation. Then when life's storms come, God will help us, even if we fall, to stand again.

What do we see Jesus do, in his own life on earth, to stay close to his Father and to maintain his own strength and resilience for the challenges he faced in his work?

EXERCISE: BUILDING RESILIENCE

Make a list of any things you have learned or practiced in these lessons that can help people build resilience through their life with Christ.

Read the following verses to identify any other practices the Bible teaches that can help us.

| Philippians 4:6–7 | Psalm 34:17–18 | Mark 14:22–25 |
| 1 John 1:9 | Hebrews 10:24–25 | Ephesians 6:7–8 |

Prayer	Philippians 4:6–7 James 5:13–16 Matthew 6:9–13
Acknowledging and grieving our losses to God and with others	Psalm 34:17–18

Reading and writing laments	Lamentations 2:18 Ecclesiastes 3:4
Music and lyrics composed, played, sung	Psalm 30:11–12 Psalm 126:2
Visual art expressions such as drawing, painting, making pottery	Numbers 21:9
Dance	Ecclesiastes 3:4 2 Samuel 6:14
Worship and communion	Mark 14:22–25 John 4:23–24 Matthew 4:10 Philippians 3:1–3
Study and meditate on God's Word	2 Timothy 3:16–17 Joshua 1:8 Psalm 1:2
Confession	1 John 1:9 Proverbs 28:13
Fellowship; close and supportive relationships with other believers	Hebrews 10:24–25 Acts 2:42 Mark 14:32–42
Accepting and extending forgiveness	Matthew 6:14 James 5:13–16
Taking our pain to the cross	Psalm 103:2–3 Isaiah 61:3
Giving to God	2 Corinthians 9:6–7 Exodus 35:29

Serving others	Matthew 20:26 Mark 10:45 Ephesians 6:7–8 Hebrews 6:10–12
Fasting	Joel 2:12–13 Isaiah 58:6 Matthew 6:16–18

These things were practiced regularly by Jesus and his followers, and his followers continue to practice these things individually and together. The body of Christ is strongest as we do the same in community (Ephesians 4:15–16). We each bear our own load, but we also help one another when our burdens are too much to bear alone (Galatians 6:2–5 and 9–10).

DISCUSSION

Share briefly which of these practices are meaningful to you and why. They may be ones you learned in these lessons, ones you already practice, or ones you would like to try.

CLOSING

Read Psalm 23 slowly. Pause between phrases for 1–2 minutes of silent reflection. Consider what God might be saying to you.

1. What am I thankful for? (Thanksgiving)
2. Are there things I regret? (Confession)
3. What would I like to ask God for? (Petition)
4. What should I do? (Response)

What is one thing you want to remember from this lesson?

OPTIONAL LESSONS

9. Coming home

Section 1. Tim's story

A few days before the squad headed home from a seven-month deployment in a combat zone, Chaplain Dave brought the team together. He reminded them that returning home after deployment was challenging. He urged them to be patient with themselves and their family members as everyone adjusted. He offered to be available in the coming months if anyone needed support.

Tim looked around, hoping his platoon would take the advice to heart. It had been a rough deployment. Three in the platoon had been wounded and two killed. Tim couldn't wait to get home and be with his family.

Three weeks later it was Tim and Sara who sat with Chaplain Dave, and Sara was in tears. Tim shook his head, trying to understand what happened to his homecoming dream. The reunion had been great. Sara looked amazing! She had prepared a special meal for the family. Everyone was excited to see him again. His son and daughter were eager to show him the new TV and introduce him to their new dog.

But after a few days Tim realized he was disappointed. He didn't expect to see such a mess in the house when he walked in. He told Sara he knew it wasn't her fault. But some of the other changes were ones he didn't expect at all. He had never been keen on having a pet, but Sara had let the kids get one. And what was wrong with the old TV? It bothered him that Sara had made such big decisions without consulting him. Even though they had contact through email and video calls when he was gone, she hadn't mentioned these things to him. When he tried to explain how he felt about it, Sara got quiet.

Over the next few days Tim began to feel that he wasn't really needed. Sara and the kids had a well-established routine, and it didn't include him. He felt more and more left out. Sara was taking online college courses in the evenings. Even though he was proud of her, he felt too exhausted and on edge to take over the bath and bedtime routines with the kids, which seemed to be what Sara expected. He found himself yelling at the kids and arguing with Sara. He had to admit he didn't feel much like talking anyway, even when they did have time together.

One night Sara cried. "Why don't you just go back?" she shouted. And the truth was, Tim wanted to go back. At least during deployment he had a purpose. He felt appreciated by his team, and they worked well as a unit. He understood what to do and he did it. Now that he was home, Tim felt like a failure. If something didn't happen soon, he was worried his marriage might not survive. At work the next morning, Tim approached his commander in the hallway to volunteer for another deployment. Chaplain Dave overheard and later asked Tim into his office.

"Tim, are you sure going on another deployment so soon is a good idea?" he asked.

"I have to do something," Tim answered. "Sara and I are fighting all the time. It seems like she and the kids are better off without me at home."

"I don't believe that, Tim. Ask Sara to come with you and let's talk about it this afternoon."

Later that day, Tim and Sara sat together in the chaplain's office and poured out their stories. Chaplain Dave listened patiently and then he guided Tim and Sara in listening to each other.

"What you are experiencing is normal," he told them. "Coming home from deployment is hard for a lot of families. We all change and grow during the months apart, so everyone has to readjust to being together again. But there are some practical things other families have found helpful for adjusting during this transition. If you and Sara can come in to meet with me, we can talk about some of those strategies and how they might help your family work through this together. Tim and Sara agreed. By the end of that first meeting, they both felt more hopeful for the future.

DISCUSSION
1. What was Tim feeling when he came home?
2. What was Sara feeling?

Section 2. What is the coming home phase of post-deployment?

A. Coming home

"Coming home" is the period of transition after a veteran's return from a deployment. It is a time to reconnect, reintegrate, and readjust relationships with family, friends, and colleagues. This phase has effects on every dimension of life—physical, mental, emotional, spiritual, and relational—for both the returning veteran and their loved ones.

DISCUSSION
1. What are common expectations people have about the coming home period?
2. How would this experience be different for people living close to the fighting who come and go from the battle lines more often?

Veterans and their families may expect that the return to life as it was before will be quick and easy. They may expect the joyful first moments of being together again to linger. But coming home is a process that takes time. It can last from several weeks to months. Most veterans and families make this transition well, but some experience greater degrees of challenge during this period.

B. Common difficulties in coming home

DISCUSSION
In addition to the difficulties the characters in the story experienced, what are other challenges veterans or their families commonly face during this period?

Common challenges that can arise during the coming home experience include:

- The veteran feeling as though they don't fit well with family and friends, or with church or other groups
- The veteran feeling lonely, isolated, or without a place to call home
- The veteran feeling on alert about their safety and the safety of loved ones
- Role confusion and changes in responsibilities for family members
- Anxiety about the next deployment
- Children feeling disconnected from or unfamiliar with their veteran parent
- Veterans and family members missing aspects of the deployment, but not feeling free to say so
- Changes in beliefs or perceptions about God, self, or others
- Loved ones feeling confused by changes in the veteran's behavior or beliefs
- Adapting to changes caused by injuries and disability

C. Common stages of coming home

Each veteran and family is unique, so each experience of coming home will be different. But the coming home period does usually unfold in identifiable stages. These will differ for each family in length of time and level of difficulty. Knowing these basic stages can help military families prepare for how things may be. One common way of naming the stages is:

- Honeymoon
- Recognizing realities
- Renegotiations
- Feeling at home again

DISCUSSION
1. What might happen in each? What might people be feeling?
2. What might make each of these stages more difficult?

Honeymoon. The veteran and loved ones reunite physically, often with feelings of relief and joy. There may be attempts to assume old roles and to pick up where they left off, as if nothing has changed. For some days or weeks there may be a focus on catching up on news, telling stories, and just being together and feeling safe.

Recognizing realities. Veterans and family members notice changes in themselves and one another, especially emotional or relational changes. Some emotions may be confusing or uncomfortable. There may be a new awareness of what was lost, such as shared events or opportunities. Family roles and routines may be different. Children may be in a different stage of development. Spouses or children may be more independent than before deployment. Some veterans may recognize that they have changed but have trouble understanding or explaining those changes to others. They may feel no one could understand, even if they could explain it.

Renegotiations. Veterans and their families begin to acknowledge losses, gains, and changes. With support and encouragement, they choose to stay engaged with one another, listen to one another, and work together to reestablish their relationship roles and routines. They also seek as a family to stay connected, or reconnect, with their extended family, community, and church.

Feeling at home again. Individual and family stability re-emerges and deepens with time, teamwork, and communication. The unfamiliar becomes more familiar. Interpersonal comfort levels return, and family tensions lessen. The veteran reconnects with valued relationships and roles with family, friends, coworkers, and in other social networks, such as church.

Section 3. What personal factors may make coming home more difficult?

DISCUSSION

What personal factors may make coming home more difficult?

Personal factors that may add challenges to the difficulty of coming home include:

- Gender
- Age
- Marital status
- Role during deployment
- Rank in military
- Injuries sustained in combat
- Proximity, intensity, or frequency of combat trauma during deployment (such as level of life threat and level of exposure to death or injuries of others)
- A history of childhood or other pre-military trauma (physical, sexual, or emotional)
- Other traumas experienced in the military (such as sexual assault or criminal assault)
- Lack of strong support networks at home before or during deployments
- Limited communication with loved ones during deployment

INDIVIDUAL REFLECTION

1. Which of these factors affected your coming home in a specific way? Were there others for you?
2. How might the experience of coming home be different for single veterans than those who are married? For those with or without children?

Section 4. Where is God at work during the coming home process?

God is always at work in our personal suffering. Even when we don't notice him, he is present to help us and provide support in our journey. Several stories in the Bible feature people who returned home after life-altering experiences. Exploring their stories can help us see how God worked to bring them help in their coming home with restoration and healing.

DISCUSSION

Read one of these stories together and then discuss the questions:

- **Ruth 1:1–7, 20–21.** What losses did Naomi experience while she was away from home? How did that affect her coming home experience? Where do you see God at work in her life?
- **Luke 15:11–24.** What happened to the younger son while he was away from home? How did that affect his coming home experience? How do you see God at work in his life?

What difficult or hopeful parts of these stories do you identify with for yourself, or have you observed in someone else's life?

Section 5. What can military families do to improve the coming home experience?

A. Understanding and applying key principles

Coming home takes time, teamwork, and truth. Veterans and families who understand and value these principles and learn to apply them can reduce difficulties and improve the experience of coming home.

DISCUSSION

1. **Coming home takes time.** As veterans and their loved ones adjust to being together again, it is helpful to go slowly at first. It is good to listen and observe. Avoid assuming that home will be

"like before." The length of the transition is different for everyone. Depending on various factors, it can last from a month or two to many months.

2. **Coming home takes teamwork.** It is helpful to tackle the transition as a family. Just as a veteran cannot complete the mission downrange alone, they cannot complete the coming home transition alone. Everyone needs to stick together in identifying problems and working them out. They need to support one another, relying on each other and rebuilding routines. Having fun together builds relationships.

3. **Coming home takes truth.** When family members have been separated and have all experienced different events, "home" will be different. For a healthy coming home, families need to talk about their changes honestly. Take time to identify and share the losses, gains, and changes experienced individually and as a family, both during and after deployment. This will strengthen family members' understanding and support for one another. Getting outside support can be helpful.

What are the blessings and the challenges of these principles?

B. Practicing communication skills

We are learning that good communication is essential for any team facing a challenge together. Veterans and those they love will be going through the coming home transition as a team, and will need to be able to both talk and listen honestly to each other.

Sharing difficult experiences that each person experienced while apart can be hard and uncomfortable. Here is a demonstration to help us understand some of the challenges families may experience in communicating during the coming home period.

DUFFEL BAG DEMONSTRATION

When veterans return home, they carry their possessions in a duffel bag. They also carry new experiences, big and small, that have changed them. Loved ones also carry their own suitcases, filled with the routine and transformative experiences they have had while the veteran was away. Their experiences may generate a variety of strong feelings that can be difficult to understand or share.

These are some of emotions that a veteran may bring home with them, or that they might feel as they try to settle in at home:

- **Excitement** (to be home—honeymoon phase)
- **Guilt** (for being gone so long, leaving team members on the battlefront, surviving when others didn't)
- **Resentment** (life went on at home without them, children grew up and changed—recognizing realities)
- **Bitterness** (from an injury they came home with, from events that took place, or they may want to go back)
- **Anxiousness** (having trouble sleeping or concentrating—on high alert)
- **Relief** (they made it home alive)
- **Pessimism** (nothing seems to matter compared to what they have experienced)
- **Moral injury or heart wound** (they may not want to talk about this issue)

DISCUSSION
1. What did you notice in this illustration?
2. How do these feelings affect how veterans and their loved ones reconnect after a deployment or other separation?
3. What other feelings or reactions might a veteran or their loved ones experience?
4. What types of feelings often "stay in the bag" and might be hard to share?

DEPLOYMENT TIMELINE

Creating a deployment timeline is a practical tool that can help families, friends, or small groups "unpack their bags" about experiences they had during a specific time period. The timeline can help them identify significant events they want to process for themselves. It can also help them share significant events with those they love.

Turn a blank piece of paper sideways, so it is wider than it is tall. Draw a horizontal line across the middle of the paper. At the beginning of the line, on the left, write "Deployed." At the end of the line, on the right, write "Home." Think about the significant events that occurred during your separation from home and mark them on the timeline. If it is helpful, think about your deployment month by month.

Family members and significant others can add their events on the same timeline (in a different color of ink) or can make their own timeline of events during the same period. The timeline can be used as a conversation starter to discuss what happened and why it was important to each person (like in the story when the family got a dog and TV).

Veterans should not share explicit details of horrific events with family members, especially children. Identifying a safe place and space to process those things is important so they do not have to bear them alone.

DISCUSSION

1. As you look at your timeline of events, does it give you any new understanding or perspective about what you experienced? Can you describe that?
2. If a loved one shared their timeline with you, did it give you a new understanding of their experience during the same period?
3. How do any new perspectives help you go forward together?

CLOSING

Psalm 40:1–5 (NLT)

> *I waited patiently for the LORD to help me,*
> *and he turned to me and heard my cry.*
> *He lifted me out of the pit of despair,*
> *out of the mud and the mire.*
> *He set my feet on solid ground*
> *and steadied me as I walked along.*
> *He has given me a new song to sing,*
> *a hymn of praise to our God.*
> *Many will see what he has done and be amazed.*
> *They will put their trust in the LORD.*
>
> *Oh, the joys of those who trust the LORD,*
> *who have no confidence in the proud*
> *or in those who worship idols.*
> *O LORD my God, you have performed many wonders for us.*
> *Your plans for us are too numerous to list.*
> *You have no equal.*
> *If I tried to recite all your wonderful deeds,*
> *I would never come to the end of them.*

This psalm reminds us of God's character and what our longings for home point to. It does not ignore real struggles but points us toward God's trustworthiness.

What is one thing you want to remember about this lesson?

10. Helping children and teens in military families

Section 1. Dion's story

Seven-year-old Dion was an only child. He was a happy-go-lucky, energetic boy who played well with his friends and was a good student at school. His mother Janelle served in the armed forces. He didn't have any contact with his father, so, during his mom's last deployment, Dion went to live with his grandmother in another town. This meant changing schools. He missed his friends and old routine and struggled to fit in at the new school. Dion missed his mother terribly, though she tried to call or video chat with him every week.

Three months into the deployment, Dion's grandmother suffered a heart attack. Dion was very frightened when the ambulance came to take her to the hospital. No one explained to him what was happening, but some kind neighbors called his uncle. Dion's grandmother began to recover, but she was not well enough to care for him. He went to live with his uncle's family in yet another town, which meant another new school and new friends. Over time, Dion began to fight with other children at school. He was angry and sullen, spending more and more time alone. He was also wetting the bed at night. Dion's uncle often called him a baby and yelled at him.

When Janelle returned from deployment, Dion moved back home. At first, things seemed to go well. But soon Janelle could see the changes in Dion. He was often in trouble at school and the bed-wetting continued. One day the teacher called and asked Janelle to come in. She told Janelle that she was concerned about Dion. They talked together about the behaviors they were noticing.

Finally, the teacher told Janelle she had an idea. "I wonder if it might help Dion to do some drawings?" She told Janelle that sometimes young children do not have words to express how they feel, but they can be encouraged to let their feelings out through art or play. Janelle decided to try this with Dion. That night after dinner, she sat with him at the table and took out some paper and markers. "Let's draw together," she said. "I missed you when I was away. Maybe you could draw pictures of things that happened while I was gone?"

Dion began to draw slowly, and soon he was deeply involved in his work. When he was finished, Janelle saw that he had drawn pictures of a plane and two stick figures with tears, an ambulance, and another larger figure with an angry face. "Can you tell me about your picture, Dion?" asked Janelle gently. Slowly, Dion began to talk, and then to cry. Over the next few weeks, Janelle spent more time encouraging Dion to draw and to talk about his drawings. Sometimes Dion asked her about her time away and she shared some things with him. She left out most of the details and things that would worry him. He felt closer to her through her careful sharing and it encouraged him to share more of his own experiences.

Janelle found a Bible storybook to read with Dion every night at bed-time. After the story, she would stay with him and they would talk about their day. They usually prayed together, too. Sometimes Dion would share more about things that happened while Janelle was deployed. He enjoyed this regular time together. Eventually, his behavior at school improved and the bed-wetting stopped. His grandmother also came to visit. Though she was much better, it was clear that she would not be able to care for Dion again. Janelle joined a support group for single parents in the military and learned how to make a new Family Care Plan before her next deployment.

DISCUSSION

1. How did Dion behave before, during, and after his mom's deployment?
2. What feelings was he having during those changes?
3. What do you think most helped him begin to heal?

Section 2. What are some losses or traumas children and teens experience in military family life?

DISCUSSION

1. What losses, transitions, or traumas can children (birth–12) experience in military family life?
2. What losses, transitions, or traumas can teens (ages 13–18) experience in military family life?

Frequent moves

- Family routines are disrupted
- Impact on childcare and on employment of spouse
- Uprooted community and school connections
- Concerns about constant life uncertainty

Deployment

- Extended absence of one or both parents
- Family routines are disrupted; childcare needs change
- Additional burdens on spouse add stress

Indirect or direct exposure to violence and war

- Fear of what may happen to a deployed parent
- Limited ability to communicate with the deployed parent
- Serious injury or death of a parent, friend, or loved one

Section 3. How are children and teens who have experienced significant loss or trauma affected?

Loss and trauma impact children and teens in many ways. Think about the child in the story and children or teens you might know in a military family and how they are affected by loss or trauma they have experienced. How does it show in their behaviors, bodies, emotions, and thoughts?

DISCUSSION

1. How is a child's behavior affected by trauma? How about a teen?
2. How is a child affected physically? A teen?
3. How are a child's emotions and thoughts affected? A teen's?

A. Their behavior is affected.

- They may go back to behaving like they did when they were younger. For example, children who had stopped sucking their thumbs may start doing it again. In their play they may act out something similar to the bad thing that happened to them.
- They may cry a lot.
- They may be especially upset if they lose things that matter to them (clothes, a toy, a book).
- They may become quiet and not respond to what is going on around them.
- They may do poorly at school because they cannot concentrate.
- They may refuse to go to school.
- They may not care if they live or die.
- Small children may cling to their parents.
- They may try to take on responsibility for the family and act like adults.
- They may fight a lot and be irritable or aggressive. Small children may fight with their playmates more than before. Older children may rebel against their parents and teachers more than before.
- Older children may use alcohol or drugs to numb their pain or become sexually active.
- Older children may take risks, like riding fast on a motorcycle, taking up a dangerous sport, or becoming a soldier. This makes them feel brave in the face of danger.

- Older children may hurt themselves, for example by cutting their bodies or committing suicide.

B. Their bodies are affected.

- Children who had stopped wetting the bed may start doing it again.
- They may have more nightmares and bad dreams than usual. (Small children who are not traumatized may have "night terrors," where they scream and look awake when they are actually asleep. It will stop as they grow older.)
- Their speech may be affected. They may begin to stutter, or they may become mute.
- They may lose their appetite because they are anxious, or they may eat too much to try to numb the pain.
- They may complain of headaches, stomachaches, or other pain in their bodies. They may have hives or asthma.

C. Their emotions and thoughts are affected.

- They may be fearful. They may be afraid of things they were not afraid of before. They may fear something bad will happen again.
- They may be angry.
- They may feel confused.
- They may be sad. Even though a child is very sad, such as after someone dies, it is normal for them to stay sad for a while, and then play for a while.
- They may lose interest in life. The pain in their hearts preoccupies their minds. It saps their energy for life.
- They may feel they are responsible for what happened.
- Older children may feel guilty they survived when others did not.

If a child suddenly begins showing these changes in behavior, body, or emotions, a parent should try to find out if something bad has happened to them, rather than just disciplining them.

Section 4. How can we help children and teens when a family member is deployed?

DISCUSSION

1. What are helpful things to do to prepare a family for a parent's deployment?
2. What are good ways to stay in touch with a parent during deployment?
3. What is helpful if family members are not able to communicate for some time?

A. Preparation for deployment

- Have the deploying person record themselves reading a book. The video or audio can be played back in segments during the deployment.
- Take special pictures of the family doing things together, and of the parent with each child.
- Let the child send a favorite small toy with the deployed parent as a connection.
- Prepare a digital scrapbook to go with the family member leaving.
- Have support networks available for those remaining home (family, friends, church).
- Talk about, in an age-appropriate way, what the deployed parent will be doing while away.
- Set expectations for what communication is possible (email, messages, video chat, letters).
- If appropriate, let the child's teachers know of the deployment. For teens, discuss this with them before doing so.

B. During deployment

- Plan as many calls and video chats as possible.
- Have a piece of the parent's clothing made into a pillow or toy (for younger children).

- Read a book or play a game online together.
- Send care packages with notes and pictures.

C. Stages of re-engagement

(See the Coming home lesson for more on these stages.)

- **Honeymoon.** Initial relief and joy when the family reunites. There may be a focus on catching up on family stories and events.
- **Recognizing realities.** Beginning to see and feel how things have changed (for example, children have grown and matured or struggled).
- **Renegotiations.** Beginning to adapt to new or changed family dynamics.
- **Feeling at home again.** Becoming more comfortable with changes to relationships and the realities of family life. Reconnecting with extended family, friends, co-workers, community and church

Section 5. What does our military culture say about how to help children and teens? What does the Bible say?

DISCUSSION

How do our military or home cultures influence the ways parents help their children and teens deal with transitions, deployment, or the death of a loved one?

Read the verses. Compare what they say with ways children and teens might be cared for in your community.

Mark 10:13–16	Deuteronomy 6:4–7
Colossians 3:21	Matthew 18:5–6

Jesus cared deeply for children and got angry when people disregarded them or caused them to sin (Mark 10:13–16; Matthew 18:5–6). Parents are responsible for the spiritual instruction of their children (Deuteronomy 6:4–9). The Bible warns parents against making their children bitter and discouraged (Colossians 3:21). As Christians, we should treat children like Jesus does, even if it goes against our cultural influences.

Section 6. How can we help children and teens who have experienced significant loss or challenges?

A. Going through major transitions

Transitions that affect children will include frequent moves, school and friendship changes, and even displacement (like children in war zones).

1. Reestablish routines.

"There is a time for everything." (Ecclesiastes 3:1a NIV)

Children recover more quickly from trauma and loss if they are able to follow normal daily routines of meals, school, chores, and playing with friends. Teens will need time alone and regular times to maintain relationships with close friends. Other family routines are also important, including going to church, reading Bible stories, and playing games together.

2. Begin healing from their own heart wounds.

"Guard your heart above all else, for it determines the course of your life." (Proverbs 4:23 NLT)

If parents have not healed or begun healing from their own heart wounds, it will be harder for them to help their children. Review the Heart wounds lesson to refresh your memory about how to heal.

3. Tell children the truth about the situation.

"For God has said, 'I will never leave you; I will never abandon you.'" (Hebrews 13:5)

Children and teens often know more than we think and think more than we know. This increases with the age of a child. A child's imagination may be worse than the reality. They will likely know that parents are upset and will wonder if it is their fault. Parents should share information in ways appropriate to the child's age about relocation, injury (potentially with disability), death, marital changes, and other issues. Ask children what questions they have rather than giving information that they may not want or need. Do not show them disturbing photos or describe injuries or violence in detail. Remind them that even when bad things happen, God is still with us.

4. Listen to children express their thoughts and feelings.

"You will listen, O LORD, to the prayers of the lowly." (Psalm 10:17)

Ask them to share what happened to them. If the child is old enough to give a thoughtful response, use the three listening questions—"What happened? How did you feel? What was the hardest part for you?" This is not the time to say, "Go away and play." If children have bad dreams, explain that many times people have dreams that may be frightening but are not true. Encourage them to talk about their dreams, comfort them if they are frightened, and stay with them until they calm down.

5. Be patient and gentle.

"Love is patient and kind." (1 Corinthians 13:4a)

Children who have experienced bad things may feel overwhelmed by their heart wounds and misbehave or disobey. When they are upset, they are not able to think clearly, learn, or change their behavior. Rather than correcting their behavior, it is best first to help them calm down by talking gently to them or possibly holding them. Being patient and gentle can help them become calm. Then they may be able to talk about what is causing them to feel angry, afraid, or sad.

6. Encourage play and sports.

Young children are often better able to express things through playing with objects rather than by answering questions. When children act out a bad event while they are playing, it helps them work out the pain they experienced. Parents can watch and then talk with the child about what the play was about. Teens can benefit from playing sports with friends. All children can benefit from physical activity they enjoy.

7. Encourage creative expression.

Children of all ages can be encouraged to draw, paint, or mold clay to express things they have experienced. Ask them to talk about their artwork: "I like what you drew. Can you tell me about it? And what is here?" This can give them an opportunity to talk about what happened and to express how they feel.

8. Talk about God and any questions children or teens may have about his care for them.

"You will keep in perfect peace all who trust in you, all whose thoughts are fixed on you!" (Isaiah 26:3 NLT)

Trauma can disrupt a child's relationship with God. Children may ask questions like, "Why did God let this happen? Was it my fault?" Adults should respond as gently and truthfully as they can from their own experience and relationship with God. They should be honest when they do not know an answer. We can trust God, and God welcomes our questions. Reading laments from the Bible and God's responses can bring comfort to children. Children can be shown how to write their own lament to talk to God in their own way.

Children can also share their prayer requests and be prayed for. Some verses to learn or think about that may help children include:

- 1 Peter 5:7 — God wants us to give our fears to him
- Psalm 23:1 — God takes care of all our needs
- Psalm 46:1 — God is always there as our refuge
- Proverbs 3:5 — God wants us to trust him
- Matthew 11:29 — God is gentle and patient

B. How do we know if children and teens need more help to heal than we are able to give them?

DISCUSSION

Some indicators that children or teens need special help include:

- harming other people or themselves, including suicidal thoughts, threats, or actions.
- inability to be comforted or calmed for a long time.
- persistent problems with sleep or problems sleeping alone (if older).
- losing weight.
- persistent intense fear of separation from caregivers.
- using alcohol or drugs.

Children with past experience in gangs or as child soldiers will also need special care. These children have seen many evil acts and may have learned to use violence as a way of solving life's problems. People may be afraid of them or hate them. The church can help the community recognize the pain, loss, and trauma these children have experienced. Over time, Christian counseling and loving care can help these children express the wounds of their hearts, give their pain to God, and begin to heal.

CLOSING

1. Which of the ways to help children and teens that we have discussed do you think might be helpful to a child or teen you know? Explain why.
2. What is one thing you want to remember about this lesson?

11. Sexual trauma

Section 1. Two stories

Emma's story

When Emma first met Tyler, the officer in charge of her new unit, she noticed that he was handsome. She also liked his leadership style. When he asked her out, she hesitated because he was her supervisor. She finally agreed, however, and they had a good time. As time went on, she began to feel uncomfortable around him and declined further requests to go out. After this, when they were alone, he began to make sexual gestures or comments to her. Twice when she walked by, he grabbed her and she pushed him away. He began to follow her back to her apartment after work.

Two weeks later, they were assigned to coordinate supplies for an upcoming mission. He was the team leader. Emma dreaded being left alone with Tyler, but her job assignment left her no other option. Sometimes she thought of telling the commanding officer. But as one of only two females in the unit, she did not want to appear weak. Emma also worried about the kind of response she would get from other members. Would it affect her career? After all, the military unit was very close, and Tyler was senior in rank. Emma just tried to avoid him when she could.

One night, Tyler ordered Emma to stay late to catalog supplies. He insisted on staying too. When everyone else was gone, he grabbed her and began to grope her. Emma shoved him away, hardly able to believe what was happening. Tyler pinned her down and sexually assaulted her. He warned her of bad consequences if she called for help or tried to tell anyone what had happened. "No one will believe you. Your military career will be over!" Emma was devastated.

After Tyler left, she found her phone and called a friend. "Please come and get me!" she begged. Janelle came quickly. When she realized what had happened, she said, "Emma, you have to report this! We can call the MPs [Military Police]. I can take you to the hospital." Emma shook her head numbly. Fear gripped her. If only she had been more careful. She never should have been alone with Tyler. Maybe this wouldn't have happened. What if Tyler returned? Could Janelle protect them? Would anyone believe her? If the MPs came, the commanding officer would find out and her unit members would know. She could not face the shame. Emma wanted to hide. How could she face working with Tyler again? She began to cry.

"Let's go back to my apartment and call the chaplain, Emma." Janelle was gentle with her. "You can share with him confidentially and he will help us figure out what to do."

DISCUSSION

1. Why didn't Emma want to tell anyone about what happened to her?
2. What do you think about how Janelle handled this situation?

The story of Amnon and Tamar   (adapted from 2 Samuel 13)

Amnon was King David's firstborn son and first in line for the throne. He became so obsessed with his half-sister Tamar that he became ill. She was a virgin, and Amnon thought he could never have her.

When his cousin saw how sad he was, he said to Amnon, "What's the trouble? Why should the son of a king look so dejected morning after morning?"

So Amnon told him, "I am in love with Tamar."

"Well," his cousin said, "Go back to bed and pretend you are ill. When your father comes to see you, ask him to let Tamar come and prepare some food for you."

When the king came to see him, Amnon did just as his cousin had told him. So King David sent Tamar to Amnon's house to prepare some food for him.

When Tamar arrived at Amnon's house, she prepared his favorite food for him. But when she set the serving tray before him, he refused to eat. "Everyone get out of here," Amnon told his servants. So they all left.

Then he said to Tamar, "Now bring the food into my bedroom and feed it to me here." So Tamar took his favorite dish to him. But as she was feeding him, he grabbed her and demanded, "Come to bed with me, my darling sister."

"No, my brother!" she cried. "Don't be foolish! Don't do this to me! Such wicked things aren't done in Israel. Where could I go in my shame? And you would be called one of the greatest fools in Israel. Please, just ask the king and he will let you marry me."

But Amnon wouldn't listen to her, and since he was stronger than she was, he raped her. Then suddenly Amnon's love turned to hate, and he hated her even more than he had loved her. "Get out of here!" he snarled at her.

"No, no!" Tamar cried. "Sending me away now is worse than what you've already done to me."

But Amnon wouldn't listen to her. He shouted for his servant and demanded, "Throw this woman out, and lock the door behind her!"

So the servant put her out. She was wearing a long, beautiful robe. But now Tamar tore her robe and put ashes on her head. Then, with her face in her hands, she went away crying.

Her brother Absalom saw her and asked, "Is it true that Amnon has been with you? Well, my sister, keep quiet for now, since he's your brother. Don't you worry about it." So Tamar remained a desolate woman in her brother Absalom's house.

When King David heard what had happened, he was very angry, but he did not do anything to punish Amnon because Amnon was his favorite son.

Absalom hated Amnon deeply because of what he had done and decided he would kill him. Two years later, he was able to trick Amnon and kill him. Afterward, he had to run for his life to another country to escape his father's anger. He stayed there for three years. Finally, David called for him to come back to Jerusalem. But even then, David refused to see him. Absalom became bitter toward David and tried to take the throne from him. He died in the attempt. This made King David even sadder.

DISCUSSION
1. What effects did this rape have on Tamar? On Amnon? On family relationships? On the nation?
2. What in this story shows that Tamar's family was not a safe place for her?
3. What do you think about how David handled this situation?

Section 2. What is sexual trauma?

A. What is sexual assault?

Sexual assault is intentional sexual contact characterized by the use of force, threats, intimidation, or abuse of authority, or when the victim does not or cannot consent. This includes rape, forcible sodomy (forced oral or anal sex), or attempts to commit these offenses. Specifically, rape is penetrating a person's anus, vagina, or mouth without their consent.

B. What is sexual harassment?

Sexual harassment is behavior that involves (repeated) unwanted or offensive sexual encounters or requests for sexual favors, and can be verbal, nonverbal, and physical. There is an implication (understood, but not necessarily stated) that failure to submit may threaten employment or career advancement. This creates a hostile work environment even when there is not a direct request for something.

Examples of behaviors:

- **Verbal:** sexual jokes or comments; comments on someone's anatomy which have sexual connotations; inappropriate use of terms of endearment such as "honey" or "babe."
- **Nonverbal:** inappropriate staring, winking, displaying sexually explicit pictures, screensavers, stalking.
- **Physical:** touching, cornering, or blocking a passageway. Sexual harassment in some cases leads to a sexual assault, especially for women.

Sexual harassment and assault are usually committed by someone who is known, but they may be committed by a stranger. Even during times of peace, sexual assault is a problem, but in times of war it is far more frequent. While sexual assault and harassment may contain an element of sexual desire, they are more about power and control. Sometimes the main purpose is to humiliate an individual or a community.

C. What is military sexual trauma?

Military sexual trauma (MST) refers to sexual assault or sexual harassment experienced during military service. Because it involves unique complications, it is often defined separately.

- A person may be forced to continue living and working with those who assaulted or harrassed them.
- A person may be isolated by their unit, lose support, or face retaliation.
- A person's experience may be minimized by those who do not wish to engage the difficult work of assisting a victim of sexual harassment or assault.
- A person may face difficulties with career advancement, or less than honorable discharges.
- Victims could be seen as troublemakers or disrupting unit cohesion.

Section 3. What are the effects of sexual trauma?

DISCUSSION

1. What are the effects of sexual assault and sexual harassment on female victims?
2. What are the effects of sexual assault and sexual harassment on male victims?
3. What are the effects on the victim's family?

A. The effects of sexual assault on victims

Sexual assault affects every part of a person's life and leaves deep wounds that last a long time. Because victims feel ashamed by the assault, they often keep it secret. Just because a person does not talk about it does not mean it has not happened.

Physical

- They may have sexually transmitted infections, injured sexual organs, or other physical injuries.
- They may be on alert all the time.

Emotional

- They may feel betrayed by an organization that has authority and that they have trusted.
- They may feel a deep sense of shame, dirtiness, and that there is something wrong with them.
- They may feel ruined, that they no longer have any value and are no longer desirable.
- They may try to minimize the pain, deny it, or try to forget about it.
- They may feel guilty, that they deserved it, or that they brought it upon themselves.

- They may be very sad. They may numb their feelings with alcohol, drugs, or food.
- They may try to take their life.
- They may be angry at others besides the one(s) who committed the assault. For example, raped women may be angry at all men.
- They may become abusers themselves and try to hurt others in the same way they have been hurt.
- They may have ongoing feelings of fear.
- They may be afraid to tell anyone, especially if telling may lead to being killed or bringing shame on the family.
- They may feel helpless and confused.
- They may be afraid of sex or no longer be able to enjoy it. They may begin having sex with many people.

Spiritual

- They may think God is punishing them.
- They may be angry at God and unable to trust God to protect them.
- They may think demons have possessed them.

Effects specific to female victims, which can vary by culture or religious beliefs

- They may not be able to get married.
- They may be forced to marry their rapist.
- If they become pregnant from the rape, they may consider abortion.
- It may affect where they are allowed to work, or they may be sent home from deployment or overseas assignments.
- They may be killed in an effort to remove shame from the family.
- They may believe this is "just part of being a woman."

Effects common to male victims

- They may develop symptoms of depression, anxiety, and PTSD.
- They may engage in risk-taking behaviors or substance abuse.

- They may be embarrassed and have a strong sense of shame.
- They may feel like they have lost their identity as a man.

If an adult was raped as a child, and he or she never received help, the recovery is more difficult.

B. The effects of sexual assault on the victim's marriage and family

If the sexual assault was done by a stranger, the family and community will probably feel compassionate toward the victim. If others witnessed the assault, they are likely to feel deeply troubled and to experience moral injury if they believe they should have intervened or reported the event and did not.

If the victim keeps their sexual assault a secret:

- his or her loved ones will not be able to understand why they are sad and angry.
- his or her spouse may not understand why having sex is so difficult now.

If the victim talks about the sexual assault and it was done by someone the family members know, this can lead to other problems:

- The family may not accept that the person who committed the sexual assault has done such a bad thing.
- If they believe that it happened, they may blame and punish the victim. In some cultures, they may even kill the victim.
- They may be afraid to confront the rapist, especially if the person is a respected member of the community or a high-ranking officer in the military.
- To keep the peace, they may deny that it happened and accuse the victim of lying.
- They may plan how to take revenge.
- If a married woman is sexually assaulted, her husband may fear getting a sexually transmitted disease.
- A husband may feel his wife is now polluted and no longer want to be with her, adding to her feelings of shame and isolation.

Section 4. How can we help someone heal from sexual trauma?

To help victims heal from rape or other forms of sexual assault, allow them to make as many decisions for themselves as possible. This helps restore the power and voice that the perpetrator took or tried to take from them.

DISCUSSION

1. What kind of medical and legal help do sexual assault victims need? Which of these resources are available in the military?
2. What kind of emotional and spiritual help do they need?
3. Let's think about how Janelle helped Emma in the story. What else could be done to help someone like Emma?

A. Encourage them to get medical care and legal help

Medical care

- Contact a sexual assault or rape crisis center within the military or in your area, if there is one. If the victim is considered an adult by the laws of the country, be sure to ask his or her permission. A crisis center will know the best steps to take to care of the victim.
- Get medical care as soon as possible. Even if there is a delay, medical care is still worthwhile.
- A doctor should check for infections and injuries like broken bones or internal bleeding.
- Medicines can be given immediately or soon after a rape that make it less likely that the person will contract HIV or other sexually transmitted diseases. These medicines are different from those that reject a possible pregnancy.
- If a victim finds out she is pregnant, she will need special help.
- If you are helping someone who has been harassed or assaulted within the military, know the protocol within your unit on how to report and, with permission, proceed.

Legal help

- Rape is a crime in most countries, as are many other types of sexual assault.
- Report to the military police. If the victim is an adult, they need to agree to report. They are not always ready to do this. Someone who has experience in this area can talk with them and help them decide what to do.
- Most countries require anyone who knows about the rape of a minor to report it to the police. Someone the victim trusts should go with him or her to the doctor and the military police. This provides comfort and support. Often, they are asked uncomfortable questions by the police or doctor.

B. Provide emotional and spiritual help through the Christian community

Emotional help

- Victims will need to feel safe in the place they are living and working within the military. It is a top priority to provide this safety for them after they are traumatized before they can begin to heal.
- Victims need someone they can trust to talk with that will keep the matter private. It's important for that person to be a good listener with the qualities for a listener that were covered in the Heart wounds lesson of this book.
- Victims with sexual trauma will need time, safety, and freedom to fully express all their feelings, including difficult ones like anger and doubts about God or faith. It's important for the listener to refrain from giving advice, from dismissing or minimizing what happened, and from blaming the victim.
- Encourage them to get counseling if available. Experienced professional counselors are best equipped to provide the long-term counseling victims of sexual trauma need.

Spiritual help

- Victims may blame God for not protecting them or may feel so angry with God that they are not willing to pray, listen to God's Word, or hear talk about God's love for them, at least at first. This is normal.
- Victims need people who are willing to show God's love to them. When they see that people still value and love them, they will gradually realize that they are not ruined. Spouses and family members can play a key role in this.
- Victims need to know it is okay for them to feel angry with God. He understands and still loves and welcomes them. It is better for them to be truthful about their feelings than to hide them. Eventually, they may be willing to receive comfort from God's Word and have others pray for them. Some Scriptures that may be helpful are Psalm 9:9–10 and Psalm 10:17–18.
- When victims are ready, they can bring their pain to God in prayer and ask God for healing. They should be encouraged to be specific in telling God what they lost in the sexual assault—for example, innocence, purity, joy. They can ask God to restore these things to them (Psalm 71:20–21).
- Christian communities can encourage biblical teaching that addresses the proper use of power in teaching about sexual abuse.
- Christian communities can demonstrate a willingness to appropriately discipline those who commit sexual assault or harassment.
- Christian communities can use and encourage the practice of individual lament to help people honestly express their feelings to God (see "Laments" in the Grief lesson).
- Christians can offer to pray for and with victims, as appropriate and when they are ready.

C. Support them in the difficult process of forgiveness

When God begins to heal the pain in victims' hearts, they can start to do the difficult work of forgiving those who assaulted them. This is not easy, and it may take a long time. It does not mean that the perpetrator does not have to face the consequences of their act. People can genuinely forgive and still bring the perpetrator to court. Forgiveness may not result in reconciliation. It may never be safe to be in a relationship with the perpetrator again.

If the perpetrator goes unpunished, it makes forgiving him or her even more difficult. It can be a comfort for victims to remember that God hates injustice and will avenge the wrong that has been done to them (Isaiah 61:8a; Isaiah 59:14–19).

Closing

1. What's one thing you want to remember from this lesson? Was there something in the lesson you found particularly helpful?
2. Share this verse with each other, then pray for each other.

    You keep track of all my sorrows.
    You have collected all my tears in your bottle.
    You have recorded each one in your book. (Psalm 56:8 NLT)

Addendum. What do perpetrators need?

Perpetrators need to repent of their sin and connect to the community. The church can help with this.

A. Perpetrators need to genuinely repent and demonstrate it by their behavior

DISCUSSION

What are signs that a person has begun the process of true repentance?

Honest admission

- They tell themselves and others the truth about what they have done.
- They feel remorse for what they have done.
- They take responsibility for the hurt they have caused.
- They search for the roots of their desire to have power over others.
- They confess their sin to God and accept God's forgiveness.

Efforts to repair the harm done

- If the victim is willing to speak with them, they ask the victim for forgiveness.
- They show their repentance by what they do, as appropriate (Numbers 5:5–7; Luke 3:8; Luke 19:8; Acts 26:20b).
- They accept that it takes time to rebuild trust.
- They accept that reconciliation may never be possible.

Discipline and supervision

- They make themselves fully accountable to another person.
- They accept the legal and social consequences for what they have done.

- If they are part of a church, they inform the pastor about what they have done and submit to any restrictions the church puts in place to protect the innocent.

B. Perpetrators need to experience community in a way that is safe for them and others

DISCUSSION

How could a church provide perpetrators of sexual assault with opportunities for community in a way that is safe for them and others?

Perpetrators of sexual assault need meaningful connection to community. If they are left isolated and alone, it is more likely that they will harm others again. A church can assign a team of mature members who can meet regularly with the person and disciple them.

Even if people have genuinely repented of sexual assault, churches should take measures to make sure that vulnerable people are never alone with them. This is also true for perpetrators who were leaders in the church. In the same way that Israel's priests were to be removed from leadership when they committed sin and led the people astray, so these church leaders should be removed from leadership. If they demonstrate genuine repentance, they may be able to be assigned other tasks to serve God's people, as Israel's priests were (Ezekiel 44:10–14).

C. Perpetrators need to heal from their heart wounds if they have been victims themselves.

Some perpetrators have been victims of sexual assault or abuse. They may need help such as found in Section 4 above.

12. Domestic abuse

Section 1. Ann leaves Joe

"You need to leave him!" Mary said. She was tying a bandage on her neighbor Ann's arm after Ann's husband had beaten her yet again.

Ann and Joe had been married for three years, during which Joe had two long deployments with the Army. For the first year of their marriage, Ann and Joe did fairly well, except Ann had noted that Joe could be very demanding. They were both Christians—Joe had come to Christ in recent years out of a troubled past. As a child, he often saw his father beat his mother.

Problems erupted for Ann and Joe when two things happened ten months after his first deployment. Ann gave birth to a baby boy that cried all the time and Joe was transferred to a new assignment which he found very challenging. He even began to talk about volunteering for another deployment.

Joe chose to respond to these problems by going out and drinking with his friends. When he came home, Ann smelled perfume on his clothes. He also became angry more easily, especially as he had to deal with the challenges of his new assignment.

Ann tried to do things to please Joe, but whatever she did just seemed to irritate him more. He began to shout at her a lot. To supplement their income, Ann found a part-time job and hired someone to care for the baby. This only seemed to make things worse. Joe kept telling her that she was a bad wife and mother.

One night, Joe came home drunk and hit her so hard that she fell against a table and broke her arm. Joe was beside himself as he took her to the hospital. He said over and over, "I didn't mean to do that! Please forgive me and don't tell the doctor!" Ann still loved Joe and thought that maybe now he would change, so she told the doctor that she had tripped and fallen outside the house.

For a few weeks, Joe didn't hit Ann, but his anger came out in harsh words. He said, "You're so stupid. You can't even look after the baby properly!" She began to think she should leave him for the sake of the baby, but then she thought, "How could I live without Joe? I'm so stupid. How could I earn enough money to survive? Besides, our pastor said that wives should submit to their husbands as the head of the home!" Just then, Joe apologized for yelling at her again, and they made up. Ann lived for those brief moments when Joe was kind and they got along.

Before long, Joe came home drunk again. The baby was crying when he walked in the door. First, he hit Ann hard, and then he said, "That stupid baby!" He picked up the little boy and slapped him. The baby screamed louder. Ann grabbed the baby from his arms and ran outside. Joe followed her, yelling profanities.

Ann banged on her neighbor Mary's door. As soon as it opened, she jumped inside. "Don't let Joe in!" she gasped. Mary's husband barred the door as Joe tried to bash it in. After a few minutes, he gave up and walked back to his house, kicking the neighbor's dog as he went.

Ann knew she could not go back to her house. She was scared that Joe might hurt her and the baby. Mary suggested that Ann and the baby stay with a kind, older lady she knew from church. Mary also suggested that Ann talk with the chaplain's wife, since she was a woman Ann knew and trusted. Ann agreed to both suggestions. Mary's husband took Ann and her baby to stay with the woman from church. Mary phoned the chaplain's wife and asked her to go and see Ann the next day. Ann was so grateful to have a neighbor like Mary.

The next morning the chaplain's wife listened to Ann for a long time. She told Ann that she could not take responsibility to make their marriage work on her own, because Joe had broken the vows they made when they wed. He had promised to love and to cherish her, and clearly he was not doing so. She read from Ephesians 5, which showed not only that wives are to submit to their husbands, but that husbands are to love their wives, "just as Christ loved the church and gave his life for it." This was like a soothing ointment to Ann's heart.

The chaplain's wife continued to meet with Ann, listening to her story and helping her see that the abuse was not her fault—and that she was not stupid! The church helped Ann and her baby find a place to live, and she was able to pay the bills by working longer hours at her job. Then one night Joe called and promised he had changed. Ann began to waver. Should she go back to him?

DISCUSSION
1. Why do you think Joe abused Ann?
2. Why do you think Ann stayed with Joe even though he was violent and abusive?
3. What helped Ann get out of this abusive situation?
4. How much is domestic abuse an issue in your military community or family?

Section 2. What is domestic abuse?

God calls us to treat family members with respect and kindness, but some homes are like war zones—places of domestic abuse.

Domestic abuse is a pattern of someone trying to control another family member. Abuse can be directed towards elders, spouses or partners, siblings, or children. The majority of victims are females, but males can also be victims of domestic abuse. It can take many forms:

- **Physical:** beating, choking, throwing things, kicking, and so on.
- **Verbal:** telling the victim they are stupid, unable to do anything right, and so on.
- **Emotional:** making the victim live in fear, isolating the victim from others.
- **Sexual:** forcing sexual relations on the victim.

- **Economic:** not allowing the victim to have money, food, education, medical help, and so on.
- **Spiritual:** misusing Bible verses, teaching, and prayer to humiliate, control, or exploit the victim.

The domestic abuse cycle

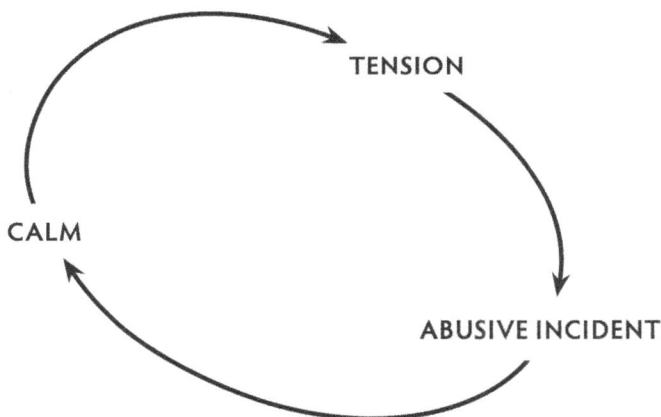

TENSION

CALM

ABUSIVE INCIDENT

All families have conflicts, but when there is a pattern of control and manipulation, it is domestic abuse. The abuse often happens in a predictable cycle: tension, abusive incident, calm; tension, abusive incident, calm.... The cycle can happen daily, or on certain days like weekends. Over time, the victim may begin to feel unable to live without the abuser and may live for the times of calm and making up. Even if victims leave the abuser, they often return.

EXERCISE: TRUE OR FALSE?

These are statements that some people believe are true while others disagree. What do you think?

1. Violence within the home is a private family matter.
2. Alcohol and drugs are the main causes of domestic abuse.
3. At times it can be helpful to beat family members.

4. A victim could stop the abuse if she or he really tried.
5. Often, the abuse stops without help from others.
6. Someone who is violent inside the home will also be violent outside the home.

(The exercise key is at the end of this lesson.)

Section 3. What do your culture and the Bible say about how we should treat family members?

DISCUSSION

1. What are expectations about family relationships within the military community that may be different from expectations outside the military context (for example, husband-wife, parent-child)?

2. What do these verses teach about relationships in the family?

1 Peter 3:7	Genesis 1:26–27	Ephesians 5:21–30
1 Corinthians 13:4–7	Colossians 3:17–21	Ephesians 4:29–32

- A husband should respect his wife and treat her with understanding because she also is an equal recipient of God's gift of life. The husband's own spiritual health depends on this (1 Peter 3:7).
- Both men and women are created in God's image and so deserve equal care (Genesis 1:26–27).
- We are each to show our reverence for Christ by submitting to one another. Husband and wife have responsibilities to each other, based on the relationship between Jesus and the church. Jesus does not hurt the church in any way. Jesus gave up his life to rescue the church from death, so the husband should be willing to do the same for his wife. He should care for his wife as he cares for his own body (Ephesians 5:21–32).
- A person who abuses does not truly love (1 Corinthians 13:4–7).
- Everything we do flows out of our relationship with God, including our family relation- ships. All family members are to relate to each other with respect, love, and kindness (Colossians 3:17–21).
- As people who belong to God, our words and behaviors should be tender and compassionate. If we are harsh and insulting, we bring sorrow to God. We are to forgive as God has forgiven us (Ephesians 4:29–32).

DISCUSSION

Do people in your community believe the Bible teaches us to treat family members harshly? If yes, what passages do they use and what do they say? Be sure to read the whole passage in context!

Section 4. Why does domestic abuse continue?

DISCUSSION

1. We saw in the story that there were many reasons the husband abused the wife. What were those reasons?
2. Are there other reasons a person might abuse family members?

Abusers may:

- have grown up in a home with domestic violence and not know how to address conflict or relate to family members in healthy ways.
- believe it is acceptable to beat family members. The culture or religion may teach this.
- feel powerless in their lives, but powerful when they are abusing another person.
- feel jealous and insecure in their marriage, fearing their spouse would leave them if they could.
- blame their actions on others.
- be experiencing symptoms resulting from a violent combat experience.
- have mental health challenges that could benefit from professional help, if available.

DISCUSSION

1. We saw in the story that there were many reasons the wife stayed in the abusive relationship. What were those reasons?
2. Are there other reasons an abused person might stay?
3. Are there particular reasons the person might stay if they or their spouse are in the military?

Abuse victims may:

- depend on the abuser for income and not be able to survive financially without him or her.
- believe they cannot survive emotionally on their own. The abuse humiliates them until they think they do not deserve respect.
- believe it is normal to be beaten, threatened, and insulted.
- believe it is wrong to leave their spouse.
- be afraid of the consequences of resisting the abuser.

- feel ashamed to let anyone know what is happening in their home. (This is especially true if churches foster the idea that Christians should never have this problem.)
- really love the abuser.
- believe they are bound to their marriage vows no matter the violence against them.
- excuse the abusive behavior by attributing it to the high stress job or responsibilities relating to the military.
- refrain from reporting abuse to avoid ending a military career and a possible dishonorable discharge.

Section 5. How can we help victims of domestic abuse?

DISCUSSION

How can victims of domestic abuse be helped? If you are a victim of domestic abuse or know of someone who has been a victim, what has been helpful?

- **Listen:** Victims need someone they can talk to, but this can be difficult because often abusers isolate their victims from contact with others.
- **Counseling:** In the beginning of getting help, **encourage the victim to see a counselor alone.** Often abusers act kindly in front of the counselor but take out their rage on the victim at home.
- **Why stay?** Ask victims, "What are the reasons you stay in the relationship?" Don't pressure them to leave but ask them about the negative things in the relationship as well as positive things. Help them recognize the cycle of abuse.
- **See effects:** Victims need to see the effects the violence is having on them and their family. If there are religious or cultural values that encourage the victim to remain in an abusive relationship, these need to be addressed.

- **Not their fault:** Help victims understand that the abuse is not their fault; it is the fault of the abuser. God sees what is happening (Psalm 10). Only the abuser can change his or her behavior.
- **Set boundaries:** Victims can decide what they will tolerate, such as, "If he hurts the children again, I will leave."
- **Prepare:** Find out what resources the military has for couples who are in abusive relationships. Some military units may even have a procedure for reporting this.
- **A plan:** They need to develop a safety plan to get out of the situation. The safest time to leave is when things are calm, rather than in the heat of a crisis. They need a place to go where the abuser cannot find them. They need practical help, such as a job and legal assistance. They may leave several times before leaving for good.
- **Healing of heart wounds:** Victims need to find healing for their heart wounds and, in due course, to forgive their abusers. The trust that has been broken can only be rebuilt over time. Abusers also need to find healing for their heart wounds which can lead to being abusive toward others. Unhealed childhood trauma, combat trauma, or other trauma may also be a factor in hurtful or abusive behaviors.
- **Church leaders address domestic abuse:** Pastors and ministry leaders can make the church a safer place for victims if they speak out against domestic abuse, offer practical assistance for victims, and discourage victims from staying in unsafe situations.
- **Churches can also build their awareness about the special strains on military families.** They can consider ways to strengthen these families under the unique challenges of military life. They can also decide how to provide special support for spouses and children during the deployment of one parent. (see Children's lesson)

DISCUSSION

What has your church done to be ready to help victims of domestic abuse? What else could be done?

Section 6. How can we help abusers?

It is not the victim's responsibility to change the abuser's behavior. However, other people can play an important role.

DISCUSSION

How might someone help an abuser change?

Some ways we can help an abuser change are to:

- Help them realize that they have a problem. Often, they have deceived themselves and blame others.
- Encourage them to get professional help, if available, from a counselor with expertise in working with abusers. Have resources ready to suggest.
- If it is safe, offer to go with them to see a person they can talk with, to help them.
- Help them deal with the root causes of their problems and find healing.
- Help them identify the things that trigger their abusive behavior and develop better ways of responding.
- If they are using drugs or alcohol, help them see the need to stop. Support groups can help.
- Help them understand that repentance includes honestly admitting what they have done, making efforts to repair the damage they have caused, and working with someone who will help them change.
- Help them seek and receive God's forgiveness for what they have done.
- Don't let them pressure a victim who has left to come back. Their behavior needs to change, and trust needs to be restored before reconciliation is possible.

Closing

Since domestic abuse is common, it is quite probable that some of you have been or are its victims. Take time now to pray for people who are living in abusive situations or who are still suffering the pain from having been in an abusive situation.

ANSWERS TO TRUE/FALSE EXERCISE
All are false.

1. Violence within the home is a private family matter.

It is sin and sin needs to be brought into the light and addressed or it festers and grows. In the majority of countries, domestic abuse is a crime. The church is called to protect people who are mistreated and powerless.

2. Alcohol and drugs are the main cause of domestic violence.

People can abuse their partner without ever drinking alcohol or taking drugs, but alcohol and drugs make abuse happen more easily, like putting kerosene on charcoal to start a fire. The main cause of domestic abuse is the desire to control and intimidate others. This may be due to not experiencing healthy, loving relationships during their childhood.

3. At times it can be helpful to beat family members.

Sometimes people use force to make spouses or children obey and submit. But in Ephesians 6:4 we read, "Parents, do not treat your children in such a way as to make them angry. Instead, raise them with Christian discipline and instruction." And in Colossians 3:19 we read, "Husbands, love your wives and do not be harsh with them." Beating may result in obedience, but it is based on fear, and it makes the home a place that is not safe or loving. To beat family members is to humiliate them and make them feel small, rather than becoming the wonderful people God created them to be.

4. A victim could stop the abuse if she or he really tried.

Only the abuser can stop the abuse. No one can make them stop. The abuser is responsible for his or her actions (Matthew 15:18–19).

5. Often, abuse stops without outside intervention.

Abusers need to face their personal problems for the abuse to stop, and most often they cannot do this without help. People do not give up power easily. Even if the physical abuse stops, the abuser can continue to control the victim without losing their temper or becoming violent, for example, clearing their throat or giving a certain look.

6. Someone who is violent inside the home will also be violent outside the home.

Abusers know how to be very pleasant in public. Usually, it's not possible to tell an abusive person from other people. For example, there have been many cases of well-respected church leaders, well-liked by their congregations, who secretly were abusing their spouses or children at home.

13. Suicide

Section 1. Caleb's story

Caleb called Pete's phone again. There was no answer. The two always met at the gym after work, but today his best friend had not shown up. After a few more failed calls, Caleb decided to stop by Pete's housing. As he drove up, he saw flashing blue lights ahead. The military police and an ambulance were in the parking area. Caleb saw Pete's girlfriend Abigail crying. Chaplain Dave was standing with her. Caleb parked and slowly walked over to them. "What happened? Where's Pete? We were supposed to meet at the gym, but he never came ..."

Abigail sobbed louder "He's gone," she cried. "Pete is gone!" Dave took Caleb aside and told him the rest of it. Pete had taken his own life with a gun he kept in his room. Caleb felt the shock like a lightning bolt. It seemed so unreal.

Over the next few days, Caleb attended the memorial service and the funeral for Pete. He stopped going to the gym and began to lose weight. He had no appetite and was finding it hard to sleep. When he did, he often had nightmares about Pete. Caleb helped Abigail clean out Pete's apartment and then drove the belongings to Pete's parents' home. Caleb knew he should stay and visit with them, but he hurried away. He felt so guilty that he had been unable to stop Pete from hurting himself. What signs had he missed? He knew Pete had been sad since returning from the last deployment He had been drinking more and talking about not wanting to be a burden on others. Their friend Jimmy had been killed in an IED explosion. Pete was not dealing well with the loss. But Caleb never thought he would do something like this.

One day, Chaplain Dave came by the battalion to check on Caleb. He asked if they could talk privately. When they were alone, he said "Caleb, I'm worried about you. You've lost weight and your commanding officer says you aren't focused at work. Your friends are worried too. We all know you and Pete were like brothers."

Caleb was quiet for a moment, and then the questions came rushing out. "Chaplain, he was my best friend! Why did he do it? Why didn't he tell me that he was hurting? I should have noticed something … I couldn't save Jimmy, and now I couldn't save Pete either." Caleb began to weep. He was embarrassed and quickly wiped his eyes with his sleeve, but the tears did not stop.

The chaplain spoke in a quiet and steady voice. "Caleb, it's okay to cry. Let it out. We may never know why Pete took his own life. It wasn't your fault. He made his choice, and we make ours." With that, Caleb broke down. Chaplain Dave waited quietly. He had tears of his own. Then they talked together for a long time. Eventually, Caleb dried his face and composed himself to go back to duty. Over the next few months, he made a point to visit the chaplain's office on a regular basis. It helped to talk to someone who knew Pete. Eventually, Caleb could think of the great memories he had with his friend rather than thinking about how he had died.

DISCUSSION
1. How did Pete's suicide affect Caleb?
2. Do you know anyone who has taken their life or attempted to do so? What effect did it have on their loved ones?

Section 2. Why do people take their own life?

Suicide is taking one's own life intentionally. It happens in all societies and by all kinds of people: young and old, men and women. In some cases, it may be unclear whether a suicide was intentional or accidental, such as when a person overdoses on drugs or alcohol and dies.

It is common to say "commit suicide," but in some cultures it is more considerate to say "die by suicide" or "take his/her own life."

DISCUSSION

Why do people take their own life?

Every case is different, but:

- Some may have lost all hope and feel there's nothing they can do to change that.
- Some may be in great emotional pain to the point that it feels unbearable. But at times they still may seem to be happy to their friends and family.
- Some may be hiding something they feel is so shameful they don't dare tell anyone. They feel suicide is the only response to shame.
- Some are convinced no one can love them and their loved ones would be better off without them.

Section 3. People in the Bible who did not want to continue living

DISCUSSION

Read the following passages about people in the Bible. Discuss what you know about the main characters.

Saul and his armor bearer	1 Samuel 31:1–6
Elijah	1 Kings 19:1–4
Job	Job 3:11–13, 24–26
Jonah	Jonah 4:1–3
Philippian jailer	Acts 16:25–28

1. What might they have been feeling? Do you think they may have been experiencing any of the common emotions/behaviors we talked about?
2. What did they do?

Examples of people who took their own lives:

- Saul asked his armor bearer to help kill him, to avoid pain and shame. Then the armor bearer took his own life, too.

Examples of those who wanted to die but did not take their own lives:

- Elijah felt despair and prayed for God to take him.
- Job felt hopeless and cursed the day he was born.
- Jonah was angry with God and wanted to die.

Example of someone who was about to take his own life, but someone stopped him:

- The Philippian jailer.

Many people in the Bible were so desperate they wanted to die, including people of great faith. Elijah, Job, and Jonah honestly expressed their wish to die to God (1 Kings 19:1–4; Job 3:11–14; Jonah 4:1–3). This did not stop God from loving them. We know that nothing can separate us from God's love. The apostle Paul writes:

> For I am certain that nothing can separate us from his love: neither death nor life, neither angels nor other heavenly rulers or powers, neither the present nor the future, neither the world above nor the world below—there is nothing in all creation that will ever be able to separate us from the love of God which is ours through Christ Jesus our Lord. (Romans 8:38–39)

We know that having suicidal feelings or taking one's life does not stop God from loving us.

Section 4. Warning signs that someone may be considering suicide

DISCUSSION

Thinking again about the story at the beginning of this lesson:

1. Why was Chaplain Dave concerned about Caleb?
2. What were some warning signs that Pete was considering taking his own life?
3. What other signs have you noticed or heard that some people show when they may be considering taking their own life?

Possible warning signs:

- They may express feelings that they are **helpless, hopeless, or worthless.**

    - Helpless: sense of inability to bear the pain
    - Hopeless: sense of being unable to stop the pain
    - Worthless: sense that they are not worthy of help or anyone's care or interest

- They may become withdrawn and isolate themselves from others.
- They may talk about wanting to die. They may say things like "What's the point of living?" or "Soon you won't have to worry about me!"
- They may give away things that are very important to them.
- They may change suddenly from being depressed to being very happy for no obvious reason.
- They may neglect taking care of themselves.
- They may begin making plans of what they could do to take their own life. (They may refer to these plans verbally or may be observed collecting medications to overdose or weapons to harm themselves.)

Not everyone considering suicide gives warning signs like this, but if they do, take them seriously. Important things to be alert for are the person feeling helpless, hopeless, or worthless. We see these feelings in many of the behaviors we discussed.

Section 5. How can we help people who are considering taking their own life?

In the story we saw that Caleb tried to go see Pete when he seemed to be struggling. What he did is a good example of what to do when we see someone like that. Even if we're not sure what they are thinking or planning, it is always good to check in with the person. In the story, Pete had already taken his own life. But what if Caleb had reached him first? How could Caleb help him? What might a helpful conversation have been like?

Caleb: Hey, Pete. I'm glad you're home. I wonder if we can talk a bit. Can I come in?

Pete: Sure. Have a seat, Caleb. What's on your mind?

Caleb: Well, I've noticed that you seem really sad since we returned from deployment. And it seems like you're drinking more than you used to. I've also heard you talking about not wanting to be a burden on anyone. It's hard to see you like this, my friend. Can you tell me what's going on? I know losing Jimmy was a hard blow for you. Is that part of it?

Pete: That's part of it. But actually, I just feel like I'd rather not be here anymore. I keep thinking about how I should have prevented Jimmy from hitting that IED. If only I had been paying more attention. I can't stop thinking about it. But it's not just Jimmy. It's all the rotten stuff we saw happen to our buddies. And for what? I'm not sure I want to live in this world.

Caleb: Man, Pete, that is really tough. I know it can rip your heart out. How bad are those kinds of thoughts for you, anyway? Have you had thoughts of ending your life? [Or, "Have you thought about doing something so that you won't have to live with this anymore?"]

Pete: (Sits quietly and nods yes) It's just that it feels too heavy and nothing's going to change. I don't want to keep dealing with it. How could it get any better?

Caleb: Sounds like you feel hopeless about it. Have you thought about how you would end your life? What I mean is, do you have a plan?

Pete: Yes.

Asking more specific questions helps you learn if the person's thoughts about suicide have become more than just thoughts. If you learn that they also have a plan and a way to carry out that plan, there is greater risk of suicide.

Pete: I'd probably use my gun. That's the quickest way to do it.

Caleb: And you have your gun here in your room?

Pete: Yes.

Caleb: Pete, would you give me your gun? Or show me where it is?

Pete: But you don't understand, Caleb. I don't know what else to do. What is there to do? Nothing is going to change.

Caleb: (Softly) Pete. Buddy. I want to help you find a different answer to this problem. I'll stay here with you, and we'll work this out together. Please show me where your gun is.

Pete: (Gets the gun and gives it to Caleb)

Caleb: I want to stay with you and make sure that you're safe. And I know that if we call Chaplain Dave, he will help us handle this. Can we do that?

Pete: (Nods his head) Yes.

Caleb: Let's call Chaplain Dave now. If he can't come over here, we can go to him just to talk. I'll go with you. Would that be okay?

Pete: (Nods yes) Alright, we can try that. But I'm not sure it's going to help.

Caleb: I know it's hard to feel like it will help, but let's just take one step at a time together. Okay?

DISCUSSION

1. What did you hear in this dialogue that might help when talking with someone who may be thinking of taking their own life?

2. What else can be done to help people who are considering taking their own life?

Listen to their pain:

- Do not avoid talking about suicide for fear of offending them or of putting the idea into their minds.
- Find out how serious they are. Have they made a plan? Have they prepared? Have they practiced? Have they thought through how this will affect others?
- Do not preach at them or tell them what to do. Instead, ask questions that will help them express how they are feeling. Tears are good. Help them find ways to release their pain and express their anger.

Keep them safe:

- If they are serious about attempting suicide, consider this an emergency and call for help.
- If possible, remove any means of suicide from their environment, like medicines, ropes, guns, and sharp objects.

- Stay with the person until help arrives unless it puts you at risk to do so.

Build hope:

- Ask them to imagine their situation being just a little bit better. What would have changed?
- Explore what has kept them from committing suicide so far. Try to build hope on those ideas. For example, if a parent is concerned about their child's future, discuss how much their child needs them.
- Find out what they have already tried to overcome their problems and help them think about what else they could try.
- Assure them that others have faced similar situations and there are ways out other than death.

Help them find additional support:

- Find out if there is a suicide hotline on the base and, if so, help them call it. Or call a military helpline to get help while you are with them. Ask what should be done then.
- Help them connect with others. Healing comes as they tell their story and reconnect with others. Even if they have professional help, they will still need the support of friends and loved ones.
- Medications for depression may help. If they are already on medication, encourage them to continue taking it.
- Help them find a professional counselor to help them.
- If there are no suicide prevention programs in your community, consider working with others to organize one. Help schools become aware that when a student attempts or dies by suicide, other students may be tempted to follow their example.

DISCUSSION

Is there anything not mentioned so far that is available or helpful to military persons or their loved ones struggling with this issue?

Section 6. How can we help loved ones of someone who has attempted to or taken their own life?

All death and loss are painful, but when someone takes their own life, the grief of loved ones is especially painful. Their lives will be marked "before the suicide" and "after the suicide." If a person attempts to take their own life but does not succeed, the effect on his or her loved ones will still be profound. Their lives will be changed.

DISCUSSION

How do you think the loved ones of someone who has taken their own life or attempted to do so may feel?

They may feel:

- guilty that they did not see the warning signs.
- guilty that they were not able to stop the person.
- angry with the person for taking their life (or trying to do so).
- stuck in their grieving process, which may be complicated and prolonged.
- ashamed, and the community may add to their shame (in some communities, for example, people who take their own life are not buried in the normal way).
- that they need to understand why the suicide happened or why the person attempted suicide.
- afraid more bad things will happen or that the person will attempt suicide again.
- unable to trust others again, particularly the person who attempted suicide.
- especially distressed if their religious tradition teaches that suicide is an unforgivable sin.
- betrayed, wondering why the person did not share his or her pain.
- angry at the military/government/leaders and blame them for what happened.
- responsible for the suicide.

Young children are more likely to think a suicide or suicide attempt was their fault.

DISCUSSION

1. When a person in your community (whether military or civilian) takes their own life, what do people do or say that is helpful to the loved ones of the deceased? What do they do or say that is not helpful?
2. How can you help the loved ones of someone who has taken their own life? If someone you loved took their own life, what has helped you?

Note: The responsibility of taking one's own life ultimately lies with that person. This is true even if others said or did things that may have contributed to the hopelessness that person felt. Other factors can also affect their emotional state and ability to cope, such as a culture of perfection in academics, bullying, influences from social media, and expectations of what it means to be a man or woman.

Ways to help the loved ones of someone who has taken their own life:

- Help with practical needs.
- Provide normal funeral services for those who die by suicide. If the suicide was in the past and there was no funeral, have a ceremony or time of remembrance for the person.
- Spend time with them.
- If the person is ready, talk openly, being careful not to shame them.
- Listen to them. Use the three listening questions from the healing lesson.
- Help them realize they are not responsible for what happened.
- Help them accept that they may never understand why the person did it. There are no simple answers for why a person takes his or her own life.
- Help them remember the good things about the person's life, not only the way he or she died.

- Encourage them to talk with a chaplain or a counselor.
- Consider a debriefing for military unit members affected.

Closing

1. Pray for those in your community affected by suicide.
2. Draw or create an image, a word art (as in the Suffering lesson), or a collage of textiles or pictures and words from magazines that reminds you of comfort and hope. In pairs, share as much as you would like and pray for one another.
3. Discuss the following questions, in pairs:

   - Have you ever known someone who wanted to end their life? How did you feel about them wanting to end their life? What did you do?
   - Have you ever been so discouraged or frustrated that you wanted to die? What was that like for you? What helped you overcome that feeling?

What is the most important thing you want to remember from this lesson?

14. Addictions

This lesson is included because trauma can lead to addictions, and addictions often cause trauma to both the addicted person and those around them.

Section 1. Maria's story

Maria could hear Mike's laughter growing louder across the room. It was the unit's annual BBQ and family members were invited to attend. She tried to pay attention to her friend Kris and the conversation they were having with the other wives, but she kept anxiously watching her husband as he finished off one beer after another. Suddenly, a voice was raised in anger, and she realized it was Mike. The other voices lowered. Maria hurried across the room to intervene.

"Give me another drink! That's an order!" Mike was slurring his words now.

"I think you've had enough, sir," said the bartender, shaking his head.

"Let's go, Mike. It's time to go home." Maria tugged at his arm firmly, pulling him toward the door. She could feel the stares and imagine the looks of pity.

When they got outside, she called to their teenage son, Alex, who was chatting with some friends. "Alex, let's go." Maria opened the door, helped Mike into the passenger seat, and walked around to the driver's side. She saw the look of disgust and shame on Alex's face and realized it was mirrored on her own.

"Gotta go," Alex mumbled to his friends, looking at the ground. He silently climbed into the back seat and Maria sped off.

Another humiliating evening, and this time in front of Mike's squad and their families. Why did she keep thinking it would get better? She had begged him for years to stop drinking, but nothing seemed to change. Now even the squad leader had witnessed his drunken behavior. Mike would surely have a hangover at work tomorrow, endangering the promotion he was hoping for. Maria sighed, wondering if things would ever get better.

The next evening Mike came back from work looking worried. For once he was not drunk and wanted to talk to Maria. "The squad leader saw me today and warned me about my drinking. I know I need to stop, but every time I think I can have just one beer, something makes me go on drinking. What can I do?"

DISCUSSION

1. What was Mike's problem?
2. What effect did his problem have on Maria and Alex?

Section 2. What is an addiction?

DISCUSSION

What is an addiction?

An addiction is an ongoing pattern of using a substance or an activity to make people feel good or help them face life. It is not easily stopped, and in the end it causes harm. An addiction differs from a habit in the following ways:

- People crave it and depend on it to face life.
- It makes them feel better, or at least keeps them from feeling pain. But when the good feeling goes away, they miss it, so they repeat the behavior again. This goes on over and over. Eventually they become unable to stop their behavior.
- As time goes on, they need to do more and more of their addictive behavior to get the same good feeling. Eventually the good feeling goes away, and people do the addiction to avoid the bad feelings that would happen if they tried to stop.

- They rely on the addictive behavior more and more and sacrifice other things to continue it.
- For chemical addictions like drugs and alcohol, the body and brain start to depend on the substance. Without it, people become physically sick. Even non-chemical addictions like sex, pornography, gambling, and gaming also affect the brain and body.
- Addictions thrive in isolation and secrecy.
- Eventually addictions destroy people's lives: their health, their families, their friendships, their jobs, and their roles in the community.

DISCUSSION

What are some things people can be addicted to?

Common addictions include alcohol, tobacco, drugs, pornography, sex, gambling, video games, social media, cell phone use, shopping, eating too much, extreme dieting, running or other exercise, and even work.

People can be addicted to things that are normally good but become harmful when these things take over their life.

Section 3. Why are people addicted?

Why do you think people become addicted?

- **Social reasons.** They are with others who drink (gamble, smoke, vape) and they want to be accepted. They need the substance to feel relaxed with other people. Family members may have an addiction, such as drinking or pornography, that influences others in the family.
- **Personal reasons**
  - They begin doing something because they enjoy it but then cannot control it.
  - The addiction numbs them from feeling the wounds of their heart.
  - The addiction may be a way of coping with stress or problems.
- **Personality and inherited traits.** Some people are much more likely than others to become addicted.
- **Early exposure.** Being exposed to an addictive substance or activity at an early age increases the likelihood of an addiction.
- **Kind of substance.** Certain substances and methods of use increase the likelihood of addiction. For example, drugs that are injected or smoked reach the brain within seconds.
- **Deployment or combat.** Additional stresses and change in life routines put service members at increased risk for addictions and other harmful behaviors.
- **Drug dependency.** This can develop following treatment for severe injuries in combat or other activities.

Having one or more of these reasons to become addicted does not mean someone *will* become addicted, but it does mean addiction is more likely.

DISCUSSION
Why don't people with an addiction just stop?

- The addiction may have changed their brain and the way it functions.
- Their bodies may crave the addiction, making it painful to stop.
- They enjoy what they are doing, or they think they have a right to do it.
- They are deceived and have developed habits of lying and manipulating people to get what they want.
- They think of themselves as addicts. They have lost hope that they will be able to change.
- The addiction keeps them from feeling the pain of problems they do not want to face.

The cycle of addiction

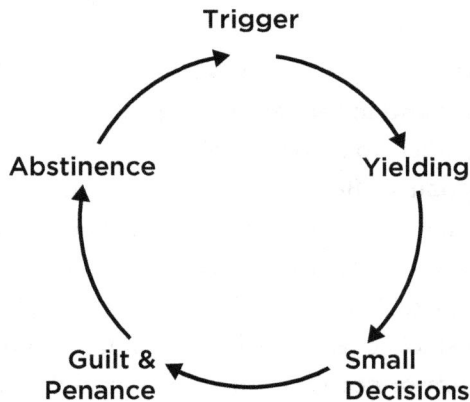

People who struggle with addictions often get trapped in a cycle. They do not always recognize the cycle or know how to stop it.

1. **Trigger:** A trigger is anything that starts the desire to engage in addictive behavior. It may include painful or positive emotions, certain thoughts or memories, stress, fatigue, or certain smells, sights, or sounds. It may even happen after a person celebrates how long they have abstained from an addiction.

2. **Small decisions:** They do something really small that opens the door to the addiction again. They feel they can withstand the temptation, or that they deserve this little thing. For example, watching television, walking past a bar or past a street corner where they previously used or bought drugs, not being honest about what they are feeling.
3. **Yielding to the desire:** They yield to the addiction again and it takes over.
4. **Guilt and penance:** They feel badly and try to do good things to make up for yielding to the temptation. They also may feel shame, feeling that something is wrong with who they are.
5. **Abstinence:** They make a commitment to stop doing or using whatever they are addicted to. During abstinence, they may feel free of their addiction, or the craving for whatever they are addicted to may begin again and can grow to become a constant internal battle.

It is possible for a person with an addiction to resist and not give in to addictive behavior. God can help them so that their desires no longer master them. God can also give them hope that one day they will be free. They will also need help from other people.

Section 4. What wisdom from the Bible can help people who are addicted?

The word "addiction" is not in the Bible. But we find there much teaching about desires, behaviors, thoughts, and temptations, all of which are involved in an addiction.

DISCUSSION

How do these verses address addiction?

James 1:14–15	Romans 6:6–7, 12–13	Ephesians 4:22–24
Hebrews 4:15–16	1 Corinthians 10:13	Ecclesiastes 4:9–12

The root of temptation is not the addictive substance (or behavior). Rather it is our desire for something that we mistakenly believe the substance will provide. As we continue to try to satisfy the desire with the substance, it can lead to an addiction. Once an addiction is formed, it is very difficult to stop (James 1:14–15).

Through a relationship with Jesus, the person we once were is counted as dead, and we are set free from sin's power. This encourages us to surrender ourselves fully to God, not to the desires of our old self (Romans 6:6–7, 12–13).

As Christians we have been given a new nature. The Holy Spirit can give us new thoughts and attitudes that are consistent with this nature. We need to get rid of the patterns of behavior from our old nature, like lying and lust (Ephesians 4:22–24 NLT).

Jesus does not condemn us for our weaknesses but feels sympathy for us. He understands what it is like to be tempted. When we are tempted, he will help us if we ask him (Hebrews 4:15–16).

God can help us resist temptations to addictive behaviors. He will ensure there is a way out and will show us how to endure the struggle (1 Corinthians 10:13).

It is much harder to resist temptation on our own. We are much stronger when we have the support of other people (Ecclesiastes 4:9–12).

Section 5. How can we help people with an addiction?

People go through stages in their willingness to deal with their addiction, and each stage requires a different response from someone who wants to help them. It is not helpful to preach to people with an addiction or try to solve their problems for them. They need to decide for themselves that they want to stop.

The stages of addiction

STAGE 1
I don't have
a problem

>

STAGE 2
Maybe I do have
a problem

>

STAGE 3
I have a problem;
I'm stopping

>

STAGE 4
Oh no!
I did it again!

ADDICTIONS SKIT

This skit gives ideas of how to respond to people at different stages of dealing with their addiction. The conversations are put together from responses that might be helpful over a period of time.

A = Person with an addiction. F = Friend

Stage 1: "I don't really have a problem." (Not ready)

F: Hi Joe, how are you?

A: Fine. Everything is going okay.

F: Really? You look pretty worn out. I heard about the party this weekend.

A: It was great! I only remember some of it, but it was fun!

F: Joe, I'm concerned about you. It seems like you've been doing this every weekend for a while. I think …

A: (interrupting) No big deal. Things are fine. See you later?

F: Hear me out. I want you to know why I'm concerned about your drinking. I'm worried how far it's going—like when you black out. It's also affecting your work and your family, and I know you care about them.

A: Really, there's nothing to worry about. Bye!

Helpful responses at Stage 1: Help them think about where their lifestyle will lead and if this is what they really want.

Stage 2: "Maybe I do have a problem." (Getting ready)

F: Hey, Joe, how are you doing?

A: Uh, okay, I guess.

F: What's going on?

A: Nothing really. I mean, this morning I woke up in a strange place and I can't remember what happened last night. I feel terrible today. It's kind of scary.

F: Yes, that does sound frightening.

A: Maybe I need to slow down a bit. Maybe not drink for a little while.

F: It'll be hard, but it sounds like a good idea. How do you think it would help?

A: Well, I wouldn't be hung over every weekend, and I'd be able to get to work on time. I probably wouldn't have so many fights at home.

F: That sounds really positive. And no more blackouts! Remember, I'm here for you. Give me a call anytime you're tempted to drink.

Helpful responses at stage 2: Help them think of the benefits and difficulties of giving up their addiction.

Stage 3: "I have a problem. I'm stopping." (Ready)

F: Joe, how are things?

A: Not good. You know I told you I was thinking of slowing down on the drinking?

F: Yeah, I remember that.

A: Well, I've tried slowing down, but it's not working. I'm out of control. I want to stop now, and I need help.

F: Thanks for telling me. This sounds really hard, but I want to help. Let's go have coffee … Why do you think you started in the first place?

A: I don't know. I was in high school, and my dad left my mom, and I was so angry, and then my friends, well, they drank pretty heavily.

F: So last week, what happened when you started drinking again? What was going on?

A: It was right after I had a fight with my dad. I was so angry I didn't know what to do.

F: Huh. Maybe you drink when you're angry and confused?

A: You know, that's true.

F: A friend of mine, Sally, got over an addiction. She said that when the craving hit, she waited ten minutes, tried to understand what she was feeling, and then did something to resist the temptation. Is there something good you can do when you start wanting a drink? I wonder if we could make a list.

A: Okay, well I could go running. Or take a walk. That usually makes me feel good. Or maybe, um, I could call you! I should skip television—all those beer ads!

F: That's a good start! Maybe we can find a support group, too. Would you like to meet Sally?

A: Sure. Good idea. That might help.

Helpful responses at stage 3: Praise the steps they are taking to stop their addiction, even the small steps. Encourage them often. Help them:

1. Pay attention to the roots of their addiction:

- Begin to pay attention to their desires, thoughts, and feelings. Explore why the addiction started in the first place.
- Address the wounds of their hearts and bring their pain to Christ for healing.
- Ask God and others to forgive them for the problems they have brought about, and then accept the full forgiveness Christ has promised.

2. Establish new habits:

- Pause when tempted and ask, "Am I hungry? Am I angry? Am I lonely? Am I tired?" This gives them a chance to evaluate why they are tempted. (In English, this spells "HALT": Hungry, Angry, Lonely, Tired.)

- Avoid situations and places where they have yielded to their addiction in the past. For example, if they went to a bar with friends thinking they would order a soft drink but ended up drunk, they should avoid places where alcohol is prominent. Or if they are addicted to gaming, set bedtime routines to avoid gaming through the night.
- Have a plan for what to do whenever they think of giving in to the addiction. Often they are able to resist if they wait, get involved in an alternate activity, or talk with someone who understands their craving.
- Replace the addiction with something good (Luke 11:24–26).
- Identify sources of tension and learn new ways to relax.

3. Find a support network:

- Encourage them to spend more time with other people rather than spending time alone. When they are tempted, they need to be with other people who are not addicted.
- Find someone who has recovered from a similar addiction whom they can call for help and report on their recovery progress.
- Connect with a local addiction recovery support group. Normally people will not recover from an addiction without support from others.
- Depending on the type of addiction, get medical help to support them in the recovery process.

Stage 4: "Oh no! I did it again!" (Falling back)

F: (concerned) Hi Joe, are you doing okay?

A: I blew it! I was doing so well! Then last night I got in a fight with my brother. I was so upset that I went to the bar and got drunk. I can't believe it.

F: I remember you said that you used to drink when you felt angry.

A: Yeah, and I had stopped drinking for five months! What am I going to do now?

F: You know, this is a normal part of recovery. It doesn't mean it's over. Today is the next step. Jesus still loves you and is walking with you on this journey. I am too. If you get angry with your brother again, please call me on the phone, okay?

Helpful responses at stage 4:

- Remind them that falling back is a common part of the recovery process.
- Give more support so that they know that even though they have fallen, they can get up on their feet again. (Psalm 37:23–24).
- Assure them that their behavior doesn't change God's love for them (Romans 5:8).

Section 6A. How can we help family members of a person with an addiction?

DISCUSSION
How might family and friends of someone with an addiction feel?

Family members and friends of someone with an addiction may feel angry, betrayed, trapped, deceitful (due to keeping the person's secrets), frightened, anxious, helpless, hopeless, desperate, and resentful.

DISCUSSION
How can we help the family members or other loved ones of a person with an addiction?

We can help family members or other loved ones:

- realize how much addictive behavior is affecting their lives and that their situation is not normal.

- identify and heal from the heart wounds they may have experienced as a result of the person's addictions (for example, physical or emotional abuse).
- address the challenges they face around the addiction, such as the feelings they are experiencing, differences of opinion on how to respond, financial strain due to rescuing the person, and so forth.
- take responsibility for their own decisions and hold the person responsible for his or her decisions, allowing him or her to face the consequences.
- talk to the person about the situation, cautiously and at the right time. This is difficult, so they may need help from other people. Most often, people with an addiction want to hide the problem. They may feel too ashamed to talk about it.
- adjust to life after the person recovers. Family members and friends may feel they have lost part of their identity and purpose in life after someone recovers. They may feel angry if people congratulate the person with an addiction for recovering and do not recognize how much the family has suffered through the years. They also may become aware for the first time of other problems they have that were not evident while the family focused on the addiction.

DISCUSSION

Imagine you are living with a person who has an addiction. Discuss these questions:

1. What can you actually change?
2. How can you take care of yourself?
3. What things might you do, intending to help the person with an addiction stop, that actually help him or her continue, for example, covering up what is happening?

Section 6B. How has your addiction impacted your life?

(for participants struggling with an addiction)

DISCUSSION

1. How has your addiction impacted your life or your military career?
2. How has your addiction impacted your family or significant others in your life?

DISCUSSION

1. When did you start the addictive behavior?
2. How did your addictive behavior change over time?
3. What is it like now?

TIMELINE ACTIVITY

Draw a timeline. Indicate when you became addicted to the various things you are or were addicted to. Then consider the following questions.

1. For anything to which you are actively addicted right now, what will your addiction look like in six months if it goes unchecked? In one year? In five years?
2. When you look back at the age you started doing the addiction, what happened in your life before that age? Draw a picture or write out what you remember.
3. Of the causes of addictions listed in Section 3, which one(s) do you think contributed to your addiction? Was there a heart wound that you were trying to cope with through your addiction?

1. Looking back at Section 5, at what stage in the addiction process are you?
2. What would going to the next stage look like?

Closing

Option 1: Community readiness

DISCUSSION

What assistance is available in your community or church for those who want to stop an addiction or who are living with someone with an addiction?

Option 2: For those helping someone who has an addiction

DISCUSSION

1. Have you ever been in relationship with someone with an addiction? Are you in that situation right now? What has that been like for you?
2. Draw the addiction cycle (Section 3) of someone you care about and whom you would like God to help you assist. Draw pictures, words, or symbols for what is happening at each stage. Which part of the cycle seems the most difficult for them to break?

The Serenity Prayer has helped many people struggling with an addiction: *God, grant me the serenity to accept the things I cannot change, courage to change the things I can, and wisdom to know the difference.*

Pray for each other.

Option 3: For people struggling with an addiction

CREATIVE EXPRESSION ACTIVITY

Reflect on a cycle of unhealthy behavior that you find yourself repeating. Draw the cycle of addiction (Section 3), with the addictive behavior represented in some way in the center. Draw pictures, words, or symbols for each part of the cycle in which you feel trapped.

1. Have you ever suffered from addiction? Are you addicted to something right now? Share as much as you are comfortable sharing.
2. What are ways in which you can stop the cycle?
3. Which part of the cycle is the most difficult for you to break?
4. What can you do to seek God's help to recover from addiction?

The Serenity Prayer has helped many people struggling with an addiction: *God, grant me the serenity to accept the things I cannot change, courage to change the things I can, and wisdom to know the difference.*

Pray for each other.

What is one thing you want to remember from this lesson?

15. Caring for the caregiver

Section 1. Chaplain Dave's story

Dave has worked as a chaplain for twelve years and found his role richly rewarding. It has given him purpose and direction. But it has become increasingly challenging. His last deployment, and its negative impact on the whole unit since their return home, has been the hardest of all.

Since his battalion returned, many of the men and women have been struggling to fit back into their families and communities. Chaplain Dave has spent long hours listening to the heartaches of people with troubled marriages and those who have turned to alcohol or drugs to cope with their problems. He also spends a lot of time trying to encourage and support others in the unit, like the medics, whose roles also include helping vulnerable and traumatized people.

Dave thinks that, as a chaplain, he should always be the one to support those who are hurting as well as those who help the hurting. He should always be ready to listen and help when they are in trouble. But he worries that he is not doing enough.

One of Chaplain Dave's good friends, Adam, was severely wounded in an explosion during the deployment. Dave can still remember the shock he felt when they brought Adam into the medical unit. For a while, he was afraid Adam would die. He could not bear the thought of telling Adam's wife and kids. Dave and his wife Michelle had been friends with Adam and Kris for a couple of years. Their kids were close in age and went to the same school. When Dave heard that Adam would survive, he felt relieved. But now he knows that Adam is using his pain medications to cope with the trauma and loss he is still grieving. Dave feels the weight of how to help Adam with that.

Though Chaplain Dave was not involved in combat, he feels almost as if he were. Many of the soldiers in the squad came to Dave to talk about the horrible things they saw and did. Recently he has felt more and more jumpy and anxious. He has feelings of anger he cannot explain. Now he has begun to have bad dreams. Even though the deployment is over, the bad dreams continue. Dave feels like a failure and sometimes thinks about no longer being a chaplain.

His wife Michelle has also noticed a change in Dave. He seems to have lost interest in a lot of things he used to care about. Sometimes he just sits in front of the television. He seems more forgetful and irritable. Sometimes he snaps at her and the kids. He rarely talks to her. On Sunday, while driving to the chapel, Dave was distracted by his thoughts and his car went off the road. He was only slightly injured, but the car was wrecked.

DISCUSSION

1. Why do you think Chaplain Dave is having all these problems?
2. Who else does caregiving in the military besides chaplains?
3. What kinds of roles are most likely to cause people to be overloaded?

Section 2. How can we know if we are overloaded?

DISCUSSION

1. What do we mean by being overloaded?
2. What are some symptoms of overload?

We are overloaded when we try to do too many things and have too much responsibility, without getting enough rest. Common signs or effects of overload include:

- Feeling angry or sad all the time
- Feeling tired and irritable
- Not sleeping well

- Having problems with relationships
- Becoming ill or having many accidents
- Resenting those who need our help
- Not interested in our work anymore
- Feeling distant from God, having difficulty praying or reading the Bible
- Questioning God's goodness and power
- Beginning to believe the lies of Satan about who we are and what we do

If we have symptoms of overload for a long time, we need to make changes in our life. Our own heart wounds that have not healed may also get in the way of our attempts to help others. And if we allow ourselves to become exhausted, we will not be able to carry on with the work God has given us.

DISCUSSION

Have you ever felt overloaded? Describe how you felt.

Section 3. Why is it difficult to be a caregiver?

DISCUSSION

What are some things that make it difficult to care for others?

Caregivers may face some of these difficulties:

A. Caregivers may be caring for too many people.

Caregivers may think they are indispensable to God's work and have to personally care for everyone. They may be working in isolation, without a team. In addition, the people they care for may think that the caregiver has to do everything. This can be especially true for chaplains, pastors, or priests.

B. Caregivers may be the object of people's anger.

People who have experienced trauma may feel angry. They may lash out without reason at the people around them. They may show anger toward caregivers who are trying to help. Remembering this can help caregivers not to take the anger personally.

C. Caregivers may be manipulated by people.

Some people who come with problems are not really seeking solutions. Some want to blame others and are not interested in making any changes themselves. Others may just want attention. These people can take up a lot of time. Caregivers need to discern those who really want help from those who are merely seeking attention.

D. Caregivers may find out certain things in confidence that they must tell others.

When people share their problems with a caregiver, what they say should be held in confidence. Some things, however, cannot be kept secret. These may include plans that would hurt someone, abuse of a child, or plans of suicide. Find out the things that must legally be reported in your area. Tell people ahead of time that these things must be reported to the authorities.

E. Caregivers may neglect taking care of themselves.

Caregivers may think they should be strong enough to bear heavy burdens without complaining or becoming angry. But if they don't acknowledge when they feel angry, sad, or afraid, they run the risk of spiritual and emotional exhaustion. And if they neglect taking care of their bodies by working nonstop, not eating well, not sleeping enough, or not getting exercise, they will run out of energy and may even collapse.

F. Caregivers may not have adequate personal support with mature believing friends who can listen to them and pray for them.

Caregivers will know some things about other people that they will need to keep confidential. But they need a steady, trusted group of mature Christian friends to share their own heart concerns with on a regular basis. They will be personally impacted from caring for others and listening to heavy burdens. They need help to carry the burdens of their own hearts.

If the caregiver is a professional (such as a counselor or chaplain) who needs to keep their work confidential, they would not be able to share things related to their work unless it were with other professionals in their confidentiality circle. If at all possible, it would be good for them to do that.

G. Caregivers may neglect their own families.

Caring for people takes time. Caregivers can easily spend so much time with others that their own family is neglected. Spouses may become depressed or angry. Children may feel angry that their parent has time for everyone else but them. The parent may not be at home enough to care for and instruct them. Eventually, caregivers who neglect their families will face serious problems.

H. Caregivers may experience secondary trauma.

DISCUSSION
> In the story, Chaplain Dave begins to have nightmares. Sometimes this is a sign of secondary trauma. What is secondary trauma? What do you remember about this from earlier lessons?

When we listen to people's stories of trauma and grief, we may absorb some of their pain and experience some of the same symptoms they are experiencing (reliving, avoiding, or being on alert all the time). This is referred to as "secondary trauma." It is not the same as being overloaded. A person could be both overloaded and experiencing secondary trauma.

If we have symptoms of secondary trauma, we need someone to talk with so that we can unload the pain that has been absorbed in our own hearts while walking alongside others in trauma. It is also helpful to express our pain to God.

DISCUSSION
> What is the most difficult thing for you about being a caregiver?

Section 4. How can caregivers take care of themselves?

DISCUSSION
> 1. Think about a cell phone. What will happen to it if it is never charged?
> 2. Is the time it takes to recharge it wasted or well-used?

We are God's instruments for good in the world. If instruments are not taken care of, they will break, run down, and lose their usefulness. Just as we must take time to recharge a cell phone or sharpen a knife or a pencil, we must stop and care for ourselves. Then we will be able to take care of others. When we listen to many people, the burden of all their pain can wear us down. We have to be careful not to be crushed by it.

DISCUSSION

What do these verses say about caring for ourselves?

1 Kings 19:3–8	Luke 5:15–16	Mark 1:35–39
Galatians 6:2	Exodus 18:13–23	Mark 6:31

A. Let God care for you.

The Bible gives examples of God's servants who were so tired that they could not continue their work. God gave them special care at that time. God took care of Elijah when he was tired and discouraged (1 Kings 19:3–8). Jesus withdrew from the demands of the crowds and prayed (Luke 5:15–16). God has promised to comfort us, help us, and be strong for us when we are overwhelmed. He understands that we are weak. Even Jesus got tired and sad and felt troubled (John 4:6; Mark 4:34–40; Matthew 26:36–46). Take time in prayer to know God's love and care for you.

B. Recognize that even Jesus, our prime example, did not help everyone.

When we see many needs, we may feel responsible to respond to all of them. Jesus did not heal every sick or hurting person in each town he visited. He regularly spent time alone with God, to let his Father guide him in everything, including when it was time to move from one village to the next (Mark 1:35–39).

C. Share your burdens with trusted friends.

Caregivers themselves need others who will love them, listen to them, and pray with and for them (Galatians 6:2). Jesus himself needed trusted friends to pray with and share his burdens with. He did not try to carry the burden of ministry alone. He lived in close fellowship with the disciples daily, and with the Father. He shared his heaviest burdens in confidence with his closest friends, Peter, James, and John. Caregivers should take time on a regular basis for prayer and sharing with a few trusted friends, in a small group or individually. These should be people of mature faith who respect personal information and practice appropriate confidentiality.

D. Share the workload with others.

When Moses was overwhelmed with work, he took his father-in-law's advice and selected people with whom he could share the work (Exodus 18:13–23). Sharing the workload means, first of all, giving up some of the control of your ministry. Others can begin to take some of the load from your shoulders. Even though they may do things differently than you do, they will learn how to serve, and you will no longer be the only one people look to for help. You will be able to work better if you can take time to recharge. It is good to have a balanced team of men and women from different ages and ethnic groups (Romans 12:4–8; Galatians 6:2; James 5:16).

E. Take time away from the situation.

Find opportunities to rest and get away from the difficulties and pain, even if only for a short time. Jesus and his disciples did (Mark 6:31). Sometimes it takes several days—even weeks—of rest to begin to release the burden. Developing a regular practice of setting aside work and quieting your soul makes it less likely that you will become overwhelmed by all you have to do.

Pastors need to reserve time for their spouse and children, since they are part of their ministry, not a barrier to it. A family retreat or vacation might be appropriate.

F. Take care of your body.

What are ways you can take care of your body?

- Get exercise daily. Exercise releases stress.
- Get enough sleep. Adults need seven to eight hours per night.
- Eat good, nourishing food. If money for food is limited, learn about healthy but less expensive options. Don't become so busy with work that you forget to eat. You need good food to be physically strong.

CLOSING

Take time in silence, reflecting on these questions:

1. Think about your work. If you are overburdened, what things could you let go of? What things could you delegate or share with others?
2. Do you have one or two trusted friends with whom to share your burdens and pray with regularly? If not, what could you do to change that?
3. What can you change to provide better care for yourself? What one thing can you do this week to begin?

CONTAINER EXERCISE

Sometimes we can be overwhelmed by what we have experienced but we are not in a situation where we can express how we feel. This exercise can be helpful.

If you feel comfortable doing so, close your eyes, or just look down at the floor so you are not distracted. Imagine a big container. It could be a big box or a shipping container. Imagine a way to lock the container, like a key or a padlock.

Now imagine putting all the things that are disturbing you right now into the container: big things, small things—everything that is disturbing you. You may need to think of a symbol to represent some of these things, for example an air ticket to represent a traumatic plane flight. When they are all inside the container, close it. Now lock the container and put the key somewhere safe. Do not throw it away. When you are ready, open your eyes and look up.

Later, find a time when you can get quiet. Take the key, open the container, and take out the things you have put inside one by one. You may want to do this with someone who can help you talk about these things. You may need a number of separate sessions to take out these things one by one. Do not leave them in the container forever!

TREE EXERCISE

This is an exercise for increasing resiliency. Doing this exercise when you are not under stress will help you be able to relax in times of stress.

Sit quietly and, if you feel comfortable, close your eyes. Reflect on this passage from Psalm 1.

> *Happy are those who reject the advice of evil people,*
> > *who do not follow the example of sinners*
> > > *or join those who have no use for God.*
> *Instead, they find joy in obeying the Law of the LORD,*
> > *and they study it day and night.*
> *They are like trees that grow beside a stream,*
> > *that bear fruit at the right time,*
> > > *and whose leaves do not dry up.*
> *They succeed in everything they do.*   *(Psalm 1:1–3)*

Imagine that you are a tree.

- What kind of tree would you be? See yourself as that kind of tree.
- In your imagination, look around. Is your tree by itself?
- What's the landscape around you?

Now look at the trunk of the tree. Notice it going down into the earth and up into the branches. Follow the branches way out into the leaves. If it's a fruit tree, see the fruit hanging from the branches.

Now follow the trunk down to the roots.

- Look at the roots—is it a long single root or many roots going out? Notice how the roots are anchored into the ground.
- Now watch how the root system brings water and nutrients to the roots and how those nutrients travel up the tree to the branches.

Notice the weather.

- Imagine the sun shining on the leaves, making oxygen. Imagine the tree just being there with just the right temperature and light.

- Now imagine a gentle rain slowly coming down over the leaves and going towards the roots. See the water going down, down into the roots. See the moisture being taken up into the tree.
- Now stop the rain and imagine the sun coming out again to dry the leaves.

Now imagine the tree with some live creatures—perhaps birds, or squirrels or insects going up and down. Watch all the activity.

Now there's a storm.

- Black clouds are beginning to form in the distance. The storm won't harm or destroy the tree, but the storm will come.
- The wind is picking up and the clouds are coming. The branches are shaking. The trunk is moving back and forth. Some of the leaves are falling and some of the fruit is falling.
- Now focus on how the roots are holding firm and allowing the tree to move back and forth in the wind. Let the storm go on a bit. Feel the tree moving back and forth with its roots firmly planted in the ground.
- Now the storm is slowing gradually until everything is still again. How is the tree feeling after the storm?
- Now the sun is returning. The insects and birds are coming back out again. Things are drying. Imagine the tree coming back to normal.

When the tree is still again, the sun is shining, the insects and the birds are back out again, gradually take some deep breaths and open your eyes.

About the authors

Healing the Wounds of Military Trauma is an adaptation of *Healing the Wounds of Trauma: How the Church Can Help* (2004) by Margaret Hill, Harriet Hill, Richard Baggé, and Pat Miersma, revised with other contributors in 2009, 2013, 2016, and 2021. New material for this edition was written by Pat Miersma, Stacey Sutherland, and Richard Baggé.

Pat Miersma received her master's degree in nursing in ethnic mental health at UCLA and has served as a counselor with SIL International since 1980. She served as an officer in the US Army Nurse Corp during the Vietnam conflict, including deployment to a Mobile Army Surgical Hospital (MASH) unit.

Stacey Sutherland is a crisis intervention specialist with a master's degree in counseling. She has worked in over 25 countries in disaster and crisis response and is executive director of the nonprofit Crisis Care International. Stacey served 11 years as a military spouse through multiple wartime deployments.

Richard Baggé, MD, studied medicine at Jefferson Medical College and psychiatry at Duke University. As a general practitioner, he served in the Indian Health Service in Arizona and later worked in Alaska. He taught psychiatry in Georgia before joining SIL International to work in Nairobi, Kenya. He is now retired and volunteering with SIL.

Margaret Hill received her master's degree from the University of Manchester, UK, and has worked with SIL International since 1968 in Bible translation and Scripture Engagement.

Harriet Hill received her Ph.D. in Intercultural Studies from Fuller Seminary. She worked with SIL for 32 years and with the Trauma Healing Institute at American Bible Society for ten years.

www.ingramcontent.com/pod-product-compliance
Lightning Source LLC
Chambersburg PA
CBHW060250050426
42448CB00009B/1606